The Making of a Liberal Democracy

The Making of a Liberal Democracy

Senegal's Passive Revolution, 1975-1985

Robert Fatton, Jr.

Lynne Rienner Publishers • Boulder & London

HOUSTON PUBLIC LIBRARY

Published in the United States of America in 1987 by
Lynne Rienner Publishers, Inc.
948 North Street, Boulder, Colorado 80302

Library of Congress Cataloging-in-Publication Data

Fatton, Robert.
    The making of a liberal democracy.

    Bibliography: p.
    Includes index.
    1. Senegal—Politics and government—1960–
I. Title.
DT549.8.F37   1987   966'.305   86-26106
ISBN 1-55587-010-4 (lib. bdg.)

Printed and bound in the United States of America

The paper used in this publication meets the requirements
of the American National Standard for Permanence of Paper for
Printed Library Materials Z39.48-1984. ∞

To Vanessa

Contents

Acknowledgments

This book would have been impossible without the generous support of numerous persons and organizations, both in Senegal and the United States.

I wish to thank the Institute for the Study of World Politics, the Carter G. Woodson Institute for Afro-American and African Studies, and the University of Virginia for financial assistance during the development of this book. I am also grateful for the help I received in Senegal from a number of friends and colleagues. I particularly wish to thank Professors Amadou Booker Sadji, Boubacar Barry, and Jacques Mariel Nzouankeu of the University of Dakar and Babacar Fall of the Ecole normale supérieure, for their warm support and hospitality. I owe a special debt to Boubacar and his beautiful family who welcomed me into their house with the most generous and unique friendship. I am also indebted to many political leaders of both the government and the opposition who allowed me in all openness to question their objectives, policies, and programs. They indeed demonstrated that *la palabre* is embodied in the democratic culture of Senegal.

The book would not have been written had it not been for a leave of absence graciously extended to me by the Department of Government and Foreign Affairs at the University of Virginia. To Robert Evans, its chair, many thanks.

I owe a debt of gratitude to Thomas M. Callaghy of Columbia University for his meticulous reading of the manuscript, as well as for his helpful and incisive criticisms and suggestions. Isabelle Bullyconnard, an exemplary student at University of Virginia, was of great assistance in translating the numerous

French quotations. Many thanks also to my two friends and colleagues of the basement of Cabell Hall, Alan Cafruny and George Klosko, for their cheerful intellectual and moral support. Defects in analysis, mistakes, and omissions are my exclusive responsibility.

Yet, even with all of this friendship and help, this book would have been impossible without the affection of Kathie. My thanks to her here can never fully express my appreciation for her empathy and friendship.

Finally, I wish to dedicate this book to my daughter Vanessa who had to endure the vicissitudes of her father's academic life during a turbulent year. Without her smile and love this book might not have been completed.

Robert Fatton, Jr.

1

Introduction:
The Making of Senegal's
Passive Revolution

Under the powerful leadership and guidance of then President Léopold Sédar Senghor, Senegal adopted in 1976 a new constitution that transformed the de facto one-party state into a tripartite political system. Initially engineered by Senghor, this system inaugurated a process of peaceful democratization, which Abdou Diouf, Senghor's constitutional successor, brought to conclusion in 1981. Indeed, the government recognized and legalized all political parties, provided that such parties rejected affiliation to "race, ethnic group, sex, religion, sect, language or region." In addition, parties were bound to respect "the Constitution, the principles of national sovereignty and democracy."[1] Thus, in five years and under the leadership of Presidents Senghor and Diouf, Senegal transformed its authoritarian one-party state into a full-fledged bourgeois liberal democracy.

What is needed at this point, before proceeding to any further analysis, is a definition of bourgeois liberal democracy. The term is used here to denote "(1) a representative government elected by (2) an electorate consisting of the entire adult population, (3) whose votes carry equal weight, and (4) who are allowed to vote for any opinion without intimidation by the state apparatus."[2] Such a form of government is bourgeois to the extent that it organizes, unifies, and reproduces the political and economic dominance of the bourgeoisie.

In the case of Senegal, however, the bourgeoisie is extremely weak and it has to depend on the state for its survival and continued growth. Such weakness partly explains some of the illiberal aspects of Senegal's liberal democracy. Indeed, the

1

absence of a hegemonic bourgeoisie has contributed to the massive economic role of the state, and this, in turn, has engendered the irresistible political rise of the state bureaucracy. The emergence of this bureaucratic statism has curbed the democratic elements of Senegal's liberal democracy: first, power is exercised not in the legislature but in the executive which rules supreme and unopposed; second, the three branches of government—legislature, executive, and judiciary—tend to fuse into a political monolith at the service of the president; and third, the principal channels of ideological dissemination and, in particular, the national mass media have been virtually monopolized by the governing Parti socialiste to legitimize its policies, programs, and general secretary, President Abdou Diouf. The combination of these factors has entailed a radical decline in representative democracy as real power has been concentrated and centralized at the summits of the bureaucratic system and particularly in the office of the president. Consequently, Senegal's liberal democracy is increasingly becoming a personalistic presidentialism.

In addition, the ruling class has been so severely weakened by the absence of a hegemonic bourgeoisie that it has felt compelled to resort to electoral fraud to maintain its absolute supremacy over the state and its different organs. In these conditions, the characterization of Senegal as a liberal democracy may appear odd and contradictory; yet, the term liberal democracy has been used to describe political systems that denied the franchise to important minorities and even majorities, and that tolerated high levels of fraud, injustice, and presidential authoritarianism.[3] The point here is that liberal democracy has been historically associated with the existence of multipartism, freedom of the press, and civil liberties, even when conditions of extreme political depravity and social distress prevailed. To the extent that Senegal has a multiparty system guaranteeing the free exchange of ideas and political competition, it qualifies as a liberal democracy.

The absence of a strong industrial bourgeoisie has imposed clear and obdurate limitations on the democratic nature of Senegal's liberal democracy; but these limitations are neither exceptional nor unique as they have coexisted with liberal democracy as a historical form of political representation. It is true, however, that the rule of the Senegalese ruling class has been marked by a persistent hegemonic instability and insecurity precisely because the Senegalese bourgeoisie—as a class engaged in the private accumulation of capital—has lacked the independent material base on which rests the power, maturity, and autonomy of a classical bourgeoisie. In fact, the Senegalese bourgeoisie represents only a fragile faction of the ruling class.

The traditional religious aristocracy and the bureaucratic bourgeoisie comprise the two other factions of this ruling class. The traditional aristocracy, *les marabouts de l'arachide*, owes its position of power to its sacred dominance over its peasant disciples from whom it extracts an economic surplus that reinforces further its position of power. The bureaucratic bourgeoisie represents the higher echelons of the civil service, which controls the state as an apparatus of repression and capital accumulation. The bureaucratic bourgeoisie's control of political power is the means by which it acquires economic power. The state becomes, therefore, the central organ of capital accumulation and enrichment.

The centrality of the state in the process of capital accumulation and thus class formation is due to the absence of a strong national bourgeoisie. This absence creates the terrain in which the bureaucratic bourgeoisie, by virtue of its control of the state, implants its political power and transforms it into material force. As Clive Thomas has pointed out:

> In the postcolonial situation, control of state power was the basis through which the petty bourgeoisie sought to confirm its social position as a ruling class.... In the process of consolidating itself as a ruling class, members of the petty bourgeoisie took on political roles and managerial positions in state enterprises.
>
> The emergence of this sector of the petty bourgeoisie [as a bureaucratic bourgeoisie] constitutes the most important postcolonial development in the class structure of peripheral capitalist societies. [The bureaucratic bourgeoisie's] essential features are its control of state property, its 'nonantagonistic' relationship to the capitalist class in the center countries, and its reinforcement of the reproduction of capitalist relations, both locally and on a world scale.
>
> .... [Thus,] in the periphery ... economic power is consolidated after political power and the state machinery are seized. This development suggests the concept of a 'state for itself'—that is, a situation in which the people occupying positions of power in the state use it to promote the economic interests of their group.[4]

State power is, therefore, the means by which the bureaucratic bourgeoisie acquires the material base required for its emergence as the dominant faction of the ruling class. Class power in peripheral societies is state power. Not surprisingly then, the bureaucratic bourgeoisie represents the dominant bloc of the Senegalese ruling class. Its control of the state allows it to accumulate political and material resources with which it can both aspire to become a real bourgeoisie and expand its dominance over the other segments of the ruling bloc. This dominance, however, is restrained by the hard realities of economic dependence on alien forces. The Senegalese state is indeed a dependent state whose subordinate and peripheral position in the world system limits its political autonomy and curbs the nationalist pretensions of its ruling class. This dependence, nonetheless, implies neither that the Senegalese ruling class is a powerless instrument of imperialist centers, nor that the Senegalese state is the mere transmissive belt of foreign capitalist interests. In fact, as this book demonstrates, the Senegalese ruling class has its own hegemonic project, a project that reflects both internal relations of forces and the quest for the resolution of a persisting organic crisis stemming from domestic class struggles.

The penetration of the capitalist mode of production into Senegal has not obliterated the specifically Senegalese modes of domination and representation. It is within this Senegalese matrix that the activities, programs, and aspirations of Senegal's ruling class must be understood. That financial, technological, and military dependence impinges on the projects of this ruling class symbolizes not its political surrender to foreign interests, but further limitations to its autonomy and power. Dependence, however, implies more than limitations; it generates also a pattern of alliances and compromises based on a coincidence of interests between the Senegalese ruling class and external capitalist agents. It is true that such alliances and compromises impose obdurate constraints on the decisions and actions of the Senegalese ruling class, but they do not erase the primacy of domestic class struggles and social practices in the shaping of Senegal's political economy.

Viewing the internal social structure as the determining explanatory arena means rejecting the notion that peripheral ruling classes are mere instruments of imperialist centers. The historical reality of dependence is taken for granted, but it

is subordinated to the complex and contradictory quest of these
ruling classes for political hegemony and autonomy. African
ruling classes have their own project of self-aggrandizement,
even if this project has exhibited two contradictory trends:
nationalism and internationalism,[5] and even if it has not been
altogether successful.[6] Thus, when African ruling classes enter
into relations of dependence it is not necessarily because they
succumb to the inherent forces of imperialism, but rather
because their interests and values tend to coincide with those
embodied in these forces. Timothy Shaw emphasizes that

> dependence needs to be reconceptualised as unequal relations
> between classes rather than countries; and underdevelopment
> needs to be reconceptualised so that uneven growth and
> distinctive class forms are recognised at the periphery. In short,
> African states are not robots that merely react to 'external' inputs
> and instructions. Rather ... structural linkages exist between
> social formations in the periphery and those in the centre;
> incorporation consists of a continuous 'transnational'
> relationship.[7]

It is in this perspective of coincidence of interests with alien
capitalist forces, and of domestic class struggles and practices,
that the Senegalese ruling class's quest for hegemony must be
understood. Such a configuration of local and external factors
inevitably implies that the dominance of this ruling class is
neither unilateral nor absolute. This dominance that seeks to
represent itself as the embodiment of the general interest rests
on an unstable equilibrium of compromises; these are required
to the extent that ruling classes must make certain concessions
and sacrifices if they are to establish and maintain their
hegemony and obtain the passive or active consent of the
subordinate classes. Because these concessions adversely affect
and constrain the ruling classes, they create an equilibrium of
forces; but it is an equilibrium that is decidedly lopsided in
favor of these ruling classes as it is always contained within the
limits of the system of bourgeois power. Such limits, however,
are quite unstable since their elasticity and expansiveness are a
function of the overall political and economic conjuncture.[8]

The unstable equilibrium of compromises characterizing
bourgeois liberal democracy creates the conditions for the
relative autonomy of the state from direct and total ruling class
control. Such relative autonomy is necessary precisely because
compromises have to be made in order to establish an

equilibrium of forces in an unstable political context in which different factions of the ruling class have different and conflicting interests. Ralph Miliband explains that

> the relative independence of the state does not reduce its class character: on the contrary, its relative independence makes it possible for the state to play its class role in an appropriately flexible manner. If it really was the simple 'instrument' of the 'ruling class,' it would be fatally inhibited in the performance of its role. Its agents absolutely need a measure of freedom in deciding how best to serve the existing social order....
>
> Reform has been a major characteristic of capitalist regimes—not surprisingly since reform has been a sine qua non of their perpetuation. What is perhaps less obvious is that it is the state upon which has fallen the prime responsibility for the organization of reform. Power-holders inside the state system have been well aware of the responsibility, and have acted upon that awareness, not because they were opposed to capitalism, but because they wanted to maintain it.
>
> But to act as the organizers of reform, power-holders have needed some elbow room, an area of political maneouvre in which statecraft in its literal sense could be exercised. What to concede and when to concede—the two being closely related—are matters of some delicacy, which a ruling class, with its eyes fixed on immediate interests and demands, cannot be expected to handle properly.[9]

The process of reform required for the ushering in and the continued survival of liberal democracy necessitates the relative autonomy of the state. Without it, the democratization of class rule is impossible. It is in this context that the transformation of Senegal's authoritarian one-party state into a multiparty liberal democracy must be understood. The significance of such a transformation derives from the fact that it crystallized in a dependent and materially backward society on the verge of economic collapse [10] and in the prevailing African and Third World contexts of developmental dictatorships and one-party states.[11]

This book is a study of the Senegalese process of liberalization. It seeks to analyze the political and social causes and consequences of this process. It also attempts to place the Senegalese experience in theoretical perspective and to demonstrate the limitations of the dominant explanatory paradigms of the making and breakdown of bourgeois democracy. Furthermore, this study assesses critically the relevance for other dependent underdeveloped nations of the Senegalese *ouverture*. Finally, it explores the hard political and material constraints on the full flowering of Senegalese democracy itself.

A brief descriptive analysis of the liberalization process is required before situating Senegal's experiment in historical and theoretical perspectives.

Phase 1: Senghorian Pluralism

In 1976, President Senghor declared his intention to adapt the Senegalese institutional framework to the prevailing political realities.[12]   In this vein, he proposed a series of constitutional revisions that were adopted by the national assembly in March and April of the same year; these revisions, which represented the first phase of the liberalization process, ushered in a tripartite political system.   The new law designated Senghor's ruling Union progressiste sénégalaise (UPS), the de facto *parti unique* of Senegal as "socialist and democratic," and provided for the crystallization of two parties of opposition.   The Parti démocratique sénégalais (PDS) of Abdoulaye Wade was constitutionally forced to be on the right of the UPS and adhere to the "liberal and democratic" creed, while the Parti africain de l'indépendance (PAI) of Majhemout Diop had the constitutional obligation of espousing the "Marxist-Leninist or Communist" ideology.[13]

The striking elements of the Senghorian constitution of 1976 were the rigid and binding political and ideological delineations imposed on the three recognized parties, the amazing creation through constitutional fiat of a legal Communist opposition, and the deliberate undoing of Senghor's own presidential authoritarian rule.   Let us briefly analyze these three political instances.

The ideological tags imposed on the three parties by the revised constitution implied both that any public and persistent departure of these parties from their assigned ideologies could lead to their legal dissolution, and that no other *courant de pensée* could materialize in the formation of recognized parties.[14] Accordingly, the UPS, the PDS, and PAI were inextricably locked into their respective world views. Moreover, since any ideological dynamism and trans-formation were constitutionally dangerous and potentially suicidal, the Senegalese political system was confronted with the vicissitudes of immobilism and stagnation.[15] Not surprisingly the PDS and PAI, as well as non-recognized political organizations, opposed the obdurate limitations of tripartism that significantly reduced the scope of democratic practice.

The rigidities of the Senghorian constitution generated the resentment of those illegal and unrecognized parties that demanded access to the political system. These parties, and in particular the Rassemblement national démocratique (RND) of Cheikh Anta Diop, argued that the tripartite constitution was too confining in terms of its ideological demarcations and that it thereby prevented the full flowering of Senegalese popular opinion and democratic pluralism.[16] Senghor and the government responded to these criticisms about the arbitrary nature of the revised constitution by claiming that the constitution was representative of the "ideological principles animating ... contemporary Senegal."[17] In other words, liberalism, democratic socialism, and Marxism-Leninism symbolized the fundamental political alternatives of the twentieth century, as well as the existing ideological divisions characterizing Senegal. Accordingly, in the governmental conception, any other *courant de pensée* was either irrelevant or too insignificant to warrant official recognition.

Senghor and the UPS were convinced that the limited pluralism embodied in tripartism reconciled the demands for liberty and democracy with the imperatives of political order and stability. In their opinion, neither the single party nor the exercise of unlimited pluralism represented satisfactory answers to the Senegalese reality. On the one hand, the government argued, the single party violated the principles of democracy or, at least, negated the full expression of the different Senegalese political families; on the other hand, unlimited pluralism would "constitute a mortal danger to the proper workings of democracy itself" since it would lead to chaos and *la chienlit*.[18] As Senghor remarked: "We should not multiply parties. Otherwise, we risk falling into anarchy. We must build solidly."[19] Hence, the acceptance of tripartism rested on the conviction that it preserved the democratic ideal and prevented the decay of political institutions.[20]

While the PDS accepted the principles of tripartism, it rejected the means that the government had adopted to achieve it. In an editorial in its paper, *Le Démocrate*, the PDS declared:

It is entirely normal that political life be regulated because, as we have always maintained, multipartism should not be a savage pluralism where each citizen hears voices like Joan of Arc or de Gaulle, and creates his own party. Even in competitive sports, not everyone who wishes to be a participant can become one, otherwise this would result in anarchy and there would be no game. That is to say that certain restrictions are desirable, even if we can argue about the acceptable number of political parties.[21]

The PDS never favored the establishment of unlimited pluralism; it demanded a referendum in which two major parties would be selected by the population. A Marxist-Leninist party would also be included in the PDS's scheme because of the uniqueness of its political vision and ideology.[22] In the view of the PDS, tripartism represented the best political format for an underdeveloped nation like Senegal. At its third congress in May 1980, Abdoulaye Wade declared:

We believe that one has to be irresponsible to want to institute in a young country an unlimited number of parties. If we followed the maximalists, we would need to legalize fourteen parties in Senegal today, since there exist fourteen different political groupings, each one claiming its specificity. One must be reasonable, for nothing prepares a dictatorship so well as an extreme and anarchical liberalism. Such liberalism would also facilitate the presence of parties incapable of living on their own, and thus exposed to control by foreign powers.[23]

In this perspective, the PDS opposed the Senghorian form of tripartism insofar as the selection of parties was based not on popular choice but on Senghor's presidential authoritarianism. The PDS's acceptance of tripartism and rejection of unlimited pluralism stemmed also from its privileged position in such a structured form of representation. With three parties, the PDS was assured of a leading role in Senegalese politics; the presence of more parties constituted a threat to its status as *the* party of the opposition.

Be that as it may, the Senghorian form of tripartism imparted to the political system a new liberalism that was all the more remarkable because of the legalization of a Communist party. Indeed, it appears paradoxical that Senghor's efforts to usher in a liberal democracy and maintain stability and order should have included such a legalization. As O'Brien remarked: "The deliberate [and of course presidentially inspired] creation of a legal Communist opposition party, is an oddity not only in West African terms but indeed by any international standards."[24] This oddity, however, has a clearer Machiavellian logic than the simple official explanation according to which the PAI was recognized because it represented a legitimate and fundamental *courant de pensée* in Senegal.

Although Marxism-Leninism has deep roots in the rich and partisan political tradition of Senegal, the official explanation is dubious since the PAI itself was banned in 1960 by this very Senghorian regime. A more likely cause of PAI's legalization in 1976 was the government's desire to divide the left and suppress its increasingly vocal clandestine organizations.[25] Indeed, PAI itself had fractured into several movements and Majhemout Diop, its historical leader, spent more than a decade in exile divorced from the day-to-day reality of Senegal. Not surprisingly, upon his return to the country in 1975, Diop was a controversial figure in the Marxist camp. His acceptance of legality and his recognition by the government as the symbol of Senegalese communism contributed further to the segmentation of the left.[26] Thus, by legalizing communism, the Senghorian regime succeeded in dividing it and suppressing its potential effectiveness. As O'Brien succintly put it, "a legal Communist party in obvious ways does facilitate the task of police surveillance, even if [for this reason among others] the PAI may not readily recruit much of a mass following."[27]

Be that as it may, it is still remarkable in the political contexts of West Africa, Africa in general, and the Third World as a whole that a one-party regime solidly in power should decide to legalize communism. That such a legalization should have been inspired by Senghor is all the more remarkable given his previous opposition to Marxism-Leninism and his decisive role in the banning of the PAI in 1960.[28] Moreover, during his more than fifteen years of power, Senghor had justified in the name of *l'essence négro-africaine* the monopolistic authority of his own brand of "presidentialism" and the elimination of all meaningful opposition.

Presidentialism, in Senghor's view, represented the specific form of African representative leadership; it symbolized the mystical relationship uniting the people to their chief. In a speech elucidating the concept of "Negro-African democracy," Senghor justified presidentialism in the following terms:

The presidential regime expresses the spirit of Negro-African philosophy which is based not on the individual but on the person. The president personifies the nation as did the monarch of former times his people. The masses are not mistaken who speak of the 'reign' of Modibo Keita, Sékou Touré or Houphouët-Boigny, in whom they see, above all, the elected of God through the people....[29]

In this respect, African presidentialism is a form of patrimonial rulership based on a complex and shifting blend of personalized, centralized, and charismatic authority.[30] The patrimonial ruler sees the government as his private domain. Under patrimonialism, as Weber indicated: "the political administration ... is treated as a purely personal affair of the ruler, and political power is considered part of his personal property."[31] In such a system then, "the personal discretion and the favor or disfavor of the ruler are decisive as a matter of principle and not just as a matter of fact...."[32] As a result, the personal attributes and the statecraft of the ruler are of absolute importance in the shaping, maintenance, and reproduction of a given patrimonial structure. "In such an administrative structure the ruler's purely *personal ability* to assert his will is to a very high degree decisive for the always unstable content of his nominal power."[33] Not surprisingly, patrimonial domination is characterized by arbitrariness and unpredictability.[34] The patrimonial ruler is not only the source of all law but he is above the law itself; African presidentialism as a type of patrimonial rulership entails, therefore, an extreme personification of power.

It is a personification that colors the political system as a whole. The dominant party embodies the leader's ideology and will, both of which in turn express the people's aspirations and needs. The leader personifies the party, the people, and ultimately the nation; he guides the course of politics, arbitrates conflicts, rewards disciples, and punishes foes. He makes and unmakes the law; he is the law.[35] As François Zuccarelli, a political scientist sympathetic to Senghor, points out:

The doctrine of *l'Union progressiste* is the Senghorian doctrine. The organization of the state by the UPS corresponds to L.S. Senghor's vision of centralized power. In general, the direction of the party, and thus of the nation as a whole, is in the hands of Léopold Sédar Senghor, the national leader.[36]

Senghor's presidential authority, in spite of its omnipotence, never degenerated into a crude and brutal dictatorship; he tolerated opposition insofar as it did not threaten his hegemony and did not constitute a major political threat. He became the supreme arbiter of disputes among his *courtiers* and disciples. Ruling like a king, he set himself above *la politique politicienne* by appointing technocratic experts as ministerial executives on whom he depended for advice, counsel, and the implementation of policies. Freed from the constraints of ordinary political pressures, he devoted his time to what he considered to be the noblest aspects of politics, namely foreign and cultural affairs. Such shielding from the daily routine of the political process protected him from popular criticisms and alienation. After all, if policies and programs failed, Senghor could always blame it on his technocratic and bureaucratic courtiers. As Adamolekun has argued:

> The presence of bureaucrats in large numbers in Senghor's governments provided him with a kind of personal political strategy for survival, by removing a very important and sensitive area of government from internal conflict and controversy. Not only did bureaucrat-ministers constitute a protective shield against professional politicians, they also shielded the president from excessive exposure to public criticism and indignation arising from economic failures, as he could always argue that the best available brains in the country were handling the problem.[37]

Senghor had therefore established his presidential omnipotence over a powerful structure of authoritarian power. Why then did he gradually dissolve it? Why did he decide to opt for a democratic alternative? Why did he create under no apparent serious threat to his rule two parties of opposition? In short, why did he usher in a "guided democracy" when he had presided over its demise in the past? Indeed, why was he contributing to the undoing of his own authoritarianism and presidential absolutism?

For the moment let me suggest the main reasons for these paradoxical political processes. In the first place, *l'ouverture* was a means of gaining a waning legitimacy at the internal and external levels.[38] Also, it served to divide the opposition—especially the left—through the partial recognition of its main components. Finally, after years of authoritarianism during which the structures of dependent capitalist (under)development had been firmly implanted, force had become less necessary and indeed counterproductive.[39] Tripartism symbolized the opposition's integration into these powerful structures and the displacement of the politics of force by the politics of hegemony.[40] In other words, the consolidation of the structures of dependent capitalism effected during the 1960s and mid-1970s made possible the relinquishment of authoritarianism and the rise of "guided democracy."[41] The social and economic crisis generated by these structures [42] required, however, a new "formative strategy" bent on creating a national "consensus" and a new class alignment.[43] The Senghorian constitution of 1976 was the means to that end; it represented what Antonio Gramsci called a "passive revolution."[44] But more about this later.

For our present purposes, what needs to be emphasized is that the rise of tripartism created the conditions for the semicompetitive elections of 1978.[45] These elections resulted in the overwhelming victories of both Senghor in the *présidentielles* (in which he obtained 82 percent of the vote) and of his Parti socialiste (PS)—the new name of the UPS—in the *législatives*. The PS won 82 seats out of the 100 composing the National Assembly. The PDS obtained 18 seats while the PAI failed to gain representation in the new parliament. Despite allegations of irregularities the elections marked the implantation of a real, if constrained, political pluralism.[46]

A relaxation of this constrained pluralism occured in 1979 with the introduction of a new constitutional revision. The revision terminated in the recognition of a fourth political party, the Mouvement républicain sénégalais (MRS) of Boubacar Gueye, which became the conservative opposition. Thus, by 1979, the Senegalese political system consisted of four legal parties embodying respectively the conservative, liberal, socialist, and communist alternatives.

This system, however, was contested by several unrecognized movements, which criticized the constitutional limitations to party formation and the nature and scope of the official opposition. In a paid advertisement in the French daily *Le Monde*, several hundred Senegalese intellectuals condemned the government for not legalizing the RND, and they also rejected tripartism and demanded the creation of a "real democracy":

On February 3, 1976, the members of *Rassemblement national démocratique* ... presented the statutes of their political formation to the competent authorities according to the laws and regulations then in force.

The new party was denied legal existence. In order to do this, an artificial tripartism was conceived, articulating arbitrarily three trends of thought. Artificial, insofar as it does not in any way reflect the Senegalese political reality. Even if it gives to the outside world the illusion of democracy, this tripartism is dangerous since it aims to exclude from the political system an important fraction of the Senegalese people.

Faced with this situation of exceptional gravity and conscious that the institution of a true democracy is a necessary condition for progress, we ask for the return of an unrestricted pluralism and for the immediate recognition of all the parties which have demanded legalization.[47]

In addition, the unrecognized movements and parties portrayed the legalization of the four *courants de pensée* as a departure from the form but not from the substance of the earlier authoritarianism. They characterized the official opposition as ineffective, opportunist, and ultimately loyal to the foundations of Senghor's regime.[48] Finally, these movements depicted the Senghorian liberalization as a means of diffusing the social malaise generated by the general crisis in agriculture and the virtual collapse of the economy.[49]

Nonetheless the inauguration of the politics of hegemony in 1976 and its consolidation during the elections of 1978 embodied a new pattern of governance that significantly differed from the earlier authoritarianism and presidential absolutism. Moreover, that the massive social and economic problems plaguing the Senegalese form of dependent capitalism engendered liberalization and tolerance instead of further repression and intransigence indicates, on the one hand, *la bonne volonté* of the ruling class and Senghor in particular and, on the other, both the strength and weakness of the ruling class itself. Indeed, confronted with legal and illegal pressures and with an "organic crisis,"[50] the ruling class opted for a "formative strategy" of democratization.[51] Yet, that it did so and still remained firmly in control was a symbol of its enduring power and its newly found hegemony over the Senegalese state.

It is in this context of hegemonic dominance that Senghor decided to resign the presidency on 1 January 1981.[52] Senghor's deliberate and unforced departure demonstrated the solidity of the new Senegalese constitution, the efficacy of the politics of hegemony, and the success of the passive revolution. The transition of power was smooth and peaceful, and the army rejected calls for a military coup to be followed by supervised elections.[53] Abdou Diouf, who was the prime minister, became—as provided by the constitution—the new president of Senegal.

Phase 2: The Emergence of Unlimited Pluralism

Upon assuming the presidency in 1981, Abdou Diouf was an unknown quantity.[54] He was *l'homme de Senghor* who had been living in Senghor's shadow for a decade as his prime minister. Reputed to be a technocrat rather than a politician, Diouf had a limited base of support within the Parti socialiste itself, and his legitimacy as president was questioned and even challenged by the opposition. Diouf had come to power only because Senghor had determined so and without the benefit of a popular mandate; moreover, he inherited from his mentor a worsening economic and social situation, and a political system that had yet to be fully consolidated.[55]

Diouf's task was therefore multiple: he had to gain popular acceptance, solidify his standing within his own Parti socialiste, free the country from Senghor's catastrophic economic legacy, and determine the parameters and scope of the politics of hegemony. To fulfill this multiple task, Diouf decided to neutralize the opposition by acceding to its political demands for unlimited pluralism. Not only was unlimited pluralism a means of conquering the terrain of the opposition, as well as the hearts and minds of the Senegalese people, but it indicated also a departure from Senghorism and its guided democracy. In short, it represented the culmination of the passive revolution. Moreover, unlimited pluralism represented a fertile soil in which Diouf could implant and grow his own independent base of support. Unlimited pluralism implied that the Parti socialiste had to develop a more coherent, disciplined, and honest organization purged of its most unpopular "barons" if it were to compete successfully in democratic elections.

It is in these circumstances that Diouf consolidated the process of democratization begun under Senghor and brought it to its logical conclusion. In April 1981, under Diouf's leadership, the national assembly legalized and recognized all political parties and transformed Senegal into a full liberal democracy. The elimination of the ideological restrictions to party formation was justified by the prime minister, Habib Thiam, as the means "to permit and guarantee the democratic expression of all the representative political currents."[56]

The coming of liberal democracy in Senegal was also marked by the implementation of a new electoral code. The code set the voting age at twenty-one and expanded the number of deputies in the national assembly from 100 to 120. But more important, it modified the previous electoral system, which had been based on a regional "first past the post" formula: that is, deputies were selected from the regional list of candidates who had achieved a simple majority; such a formula clearly benefited the Parti socialiste since it was the best organized, most resourceful, and best known party.[57]

The new code maintained the regional "first past the post" formula but only for the election of half of the deputies. The other half was to be elected by "national proportional representation." Both the departmental and national lists, however, would be on the same ballot paper. In this way, the code eliminated the most glaring electoral advantages of the Parti socialiste without endangering its supremacy; indeed, a bare simple majority at both the departmental and national levels would guarantee an overwhelming majority in parliament.[58] Here again, the privileges of the Parti socialiste as the ruling and best organized party would be decisive.

Not surprisingly, the PDS expressed its discontent with the new electoral code: "The combination of two methods could give three-quarters of the seats at the National Assembly to a party which won just 50 percent of the votes—all of the sixty local seats on the Departmental list and thirty of the seats on the National list. This would clearly be a great injustice."[59]

The election of the president, however, followed a different and simpler modality. The new electoral code stipulated that the president be elected in the first round only if he gained the absolute majority of the poll expressed by at least a third of the registered voters. Otherwise, a second round would take place two Sundays afterwards in which only the top two candidates could participate; the candidate obtaining the greatest number of votes in this second round would be declared president.[60] All in all, then, the new electoral code, however modified, still maintained the electoral advantages of the PS. These electoral advantages were further reinforced by the overwhelming support given by the *marabouts*—the heads of the Muslim brotherhoods—to the PS and President Diouf in particular.[61] This theme will be studied in greater detail in following chapters.

The elections of 1983 represented an overwhelming triumph for Diouf and his Parti socialiste, in spite of the opposition's justified charges of widespread irregularities.[62] Diouf was elected with more than 83 percent of the vote, while his Parti socialiste—with close to 80 percent—gained 111 parliamentary seats out of a possible 120.[63] Only the PDS of Abdoulaye Wade and the Rassemblement national démocratique (RND) of Cheikh Anta Diop won parliamentary representation with, respectively, eight and one deputies.

Poorly organized, lacking resources, and divided—into the PAI, the Ligue démocratique–Mouvement pour le parti du travail (LD–MPT), the Parti populaire sénégalais (PPS), and the Ligue communiste des travailleurs (LTC)—the Marxian left obtained a disastrous 2.17 percent of the vote.[64] As O'Brien remarked, "the extreme left was thus offered the electoral rope to hang itself."[65]

The catastrophic score of the opposition, and the left in particular, reflected a combination of factors. In the first place, widespread irregularities and fraud deprived the opposition of a much better performance. Second, having monopolized the governmental apparatus since independence, the PS became identified as the state that few voters would dare defy; indeed, only the brave in a depressed economy of limited employment opportunities could openly challenge the "patron-state," which represented the main supplier of jobs and security. Third, President Diouf's indisputable popularity and charisma contributed significantly to the high score of the PS. Nevertheless, it is clear that flagrant fraud was decisive in the making of the overwhelming PS victory. As Donal Cruise O'Brien observes:

> The exact scale of electoral distortion is impossible to assess, but reports from observers at the polls have left an impression of very widespread irregularity.... [However,] electoral manipulation was absolutely unnecessary to ensure the victory of President Abdou Diouf, a very popular candidate with an unblemished record. Chicanery was probably unnecessary to give the Parti socialiste a parliamentary majority, given the superiority of its organisation, the patronage at its disposal, the

support of so many prominent figures and its links with state administration.   But it does seem that a mood of panic overcame the *socialistes* in the last stages of the election campaign, with the unexpectedly effective challenge of Abdoulaye Wade's Parti démocratique sénégalais.[66]

Yet, in spite of the gross irregularities of the 1983 elections, the opposition was free to campaign and, through its partisan, if organizationally weak, media, it criticized the government without restrictions.   In this sense, the Senegalese democratic experience is noteworthy and, indeed, unique in the African context of military rule, single-party state, and developmental dictatorship.   The obvious question, then, is: Why has a liberal democracy been implanted in Senegal?   The following chapters will seek to answer this question.

The next chapter places the Senegalese process of democratization in theoretical perspective and reviews the main theoretical paradigms explaining the rise and breakdown of democracy.   Although these paradigms are not totally wrong, they suffer from serious limitations; they all imply the impossibility of liberal democracy for dependent and economically backward peripheral nations like Senegal. Accordingly, a better and less rigid explanatory framework is required to resolve the Senegalese puzzle.

Chapters 3 and 4 seek to develop from Antonio Gramsci's notion of "passive revolution" such an explanatory framework. They show not only that liberal democracy is possible in underdeveloped societies, but that it might represent the best vehicle for the persistence of ruling class power. In this respect, democratization unfolds as a passive revolution; a revolution that is formulated, guided, and controlled by the ruling class as a means of congealing, in the form of bourgeois democracy, the political participation, representation, and integration of subordinate groups and classes.   Passive revolutions are, therefore, processes of containment of popular aspirations for radical social transformations, and they symbolize the obdurate democratic limitations of liberal democracy.

These limitations are reflected in the programs and policies of the governing Parti socialiste, which are critically analyzed in Chapter 5.   This chapter also studies the political alternatives provided by the parties of the opposition.   Finally, Chapter 6 summarizes what has been learned, reexamining in a comparative perspective the implications of and alternatives to passive revolutions. The analysis suggests that even though there are powerful incentives for the ruling classes of dependent and peripheral societies to embark on passive revolutions, there are also profound economic, political, and social constraints for them not to do so. In conclusion, it is argued that the concept of passive revolution transcends the rigidities of the dominant analytical frameworks that have shaped the political study of the processes of democratization in underdeveloped societies.

Notes

1. *West Africa*, 25 May 1981: 1142.
2. Goran Therborn, "The Rule of Capital and the Rise of Democracy," in David Held et al., ed., *States and Societies*, New York: New York University Press, 1983, 262.
3. C. B. Macpherson, *The Life and Times of Liberal Democracy*, New York: Oxford University Press, 1977. Nicos Poulantzas, *State, Power, Socialism*, London: Verso Edition, 1980, 261–289. Goran Therborn, *What Does the Ruling Class Do When It Rules?* London: Verso Edition, 1980, 49–124.
4. Clive Thomas, *The Rise of the Authoritarian State in Peripheral Societies*, New York: Monthly Review Press, 1984, 60–62. See also Gilberto Mathias and Pierre Salama, *L'Etat Surdéveloppé: Des Métropoles au Tiers Monde*, Paris: Maspéro, 1983, 32.
5. Nicola Swainson, *The Development of Corporate Capitalism in Kenya*, 1918–1977, Berkeley: University of California Press, 1980, 17.
6. Frederick Cooper, "Africa and the World Economy,"*African Studies Review*, Vol. 29, Nos. 2/3 (1981): 20–21.
7. Timothy M. Shaw, "Beyond Neo-Colonialism: Varieties of Corporatism in Africa," *The Journal of Modern African Studies*, Vol. 20, No. 2 (1982): 241. See also Fernando Henrique Cardoso and Enzo Faletto, *Dependency and Development in Latin America*, Berkeley: University of California Press, 1979, xvi.
8. Antonio Gramsci, *Selections from Prison Notebooks*, ed. and trans. by Quintin Hoare and Geoffrey Nowell Smith, London: Lawrence and Wishart, 1971, 57–60. Nicos Poulantzas, *Political Power and Social Classes*, London: Verso Edition, 1978, 190–194.
9. Ralph Miliband, *Marxism and Politics*, New York: Oxford University Press, 1977, 87–88.
10. Monique Anson-Meyer, *Mécanismes de l'Exploitation en Afrique: L'Exemple du Sénégal*, La Rochelle: Editions Cujas, 1974. Rita Cruise O'Brien, ed., *The Political Economy of Underdevelopment: Dependence in Senegal*, Beverly Hills: Sage Publications, 1979.
11. Richard Sklar, "Democracy in Africa," *African Studies Review*, Vol. 26, Nos. 3/4, (1983): 11–24.

12. Ibrahima Fall, *Sous-Développement et Démocratie Multipartisane: L'Expérience Sénégalaise*, Dakar: Les Nouvelles Editions Africaines, 1977, 22–24. François Zuccarelli, "L'Evolution Récente de la Vie Politique au Sénégal," *Revue Française d'Etudes Politiques Africaines* , No. 127 (1976): 85–102.

13. Fall, *Sous-Développement et Démocratie Multipartisane*, 103–106. Donal Cruise O'Brien, "Senegal," in John Dunn, ed., *West African States: Failure and Promise,* Cambridge: Cambridge University Press, 1978, 173–188. *West Africa* 6 March 1978: 421.

14. Fall, *Sous-Développement et Démocratie Multipartisane*, 104.

15. Ibid., 31–49.

16. Sheldon Gellar, *Senegal: An African Nation Between Islam and the West*, Boulder: Westview Press, 1982, 37.

17. Fall, *Sous-Développement et Démocratie Multipartisane*, 103.

18. Ibid., 101. *Jeune Afrique*, 29 novembre 1978: 31–33.

19. Léopold Sédar Senghor, *Léopold Sédar Senghor: La Poésie de l'Action. Conversations avec Mohamed Aziza*, Paris: Stock, 1980, 226 (my translation).

20. Fall, *Sous-Développement et Démocratie Multipartisane*, 23. *Jeune Afrique*, 29 Novembre, 1978: 31–33.

21. Cited as quoted in Christine Desouches, *Le Parti Démocratique Sénégalais*, Paris: Berger-Levrault, 1983, 63 (my translation).

22. Ibid.

23. Ibid. (my translation).

24. O'Brien, "Senegal," 173.

25. Ibid., 180.

26. Pierre Biarnes, "A Propos du Deuxième Congrès du PAI Sénégalais (Dakar–16 et 17 février 1979)," *Revue Française d'Etudes Politiques Africaines*, No. 160: 60–63.

27. O'Brien, "Senegal," 180.

28. Irving Leonard Markovitz, *Léopold Sédar Senghor and the Politics of Négritude*, New York: Atheneum, 1969, 119–193.

29. Ibid., 204.

30. Thomas Callaghy, "The State as Lame Leviathan: The Patrimonial Administrative State in Africa," in Zaki Ergas, ed., *The African State in Transition*, New York: Macmillan, forthcoming.

31. Max Weber, *Economy and Society*, 2 Vols., ed. by Guenther Roth and Claus Wittich, Berkeley: California University Press, 1978, 1029.

32. Ibid., 1030.

33. Ibid., 1042.

34. Ibid., 1096.

35. Jean-François Bayart, *L'Etat au Cameroun*, 2nd. ed., Paris: Presses de la Fondation Nationale des Sciences Politiques, 1985, 141–159; Abdoulaye Ly, *Sur le Présidentialisme Néocolonial au Sénégal. Pour un Positionnement Objectif*, Dakar: And-Jef/MRDN, 1984.

36. François Zuccarelli, *Un Parti Politique Africain: L'Union*

Progressiste Sénégalaise, Paris: Pichon et Durand-Auzias, 1970, 116 (my translation).

37. Lapido Adamolekun, "Bureaucrats and the Senegalese Political Process," *The Journal of Modern African Studies*, Vol. 9, No. 4: 556.

38. O'Brien, "Senegal," 179.

39. Samir Amin, *Neo-Colonialism in West Africa*, Harmondsworth: Penguin Books, 1973. Pierre Fougeyrollas, *Où Va le Sénégal?* Paris: Editions Anthropos, 1970.

40. Gramsci, *Selections from Prison Notebooks*, 206–276.

41. Amin, *Neo-Colonialism*.

42. Ibid. Gellar, *Senegal*, 45–66. Rita Cruise O'Brien, *The Political Economy of Underdevelopment*, 100–125.

43. Stuart Hall, "Moving Right," *Socialist Review*, 55, (1981): 113–137.

44. Gramsci, *Selections from Prison Notebooks*, 178–181. Anne Showstack Sassoon, "Passive Revolution and the Politics of Reform," in Anne Showstack Sassoon, ed., *Approaches to Gramsci*, London: Writers and Readers, 1982.

45. *West Africa*, 20 February 1978: 327; 6 March 1978: 421.

46. Ibid.

47. *Le Monde*, 16 septembre 1977: 8 (my translation).

48. *West Africa*, 20 February 1978: 327.

49. René Dumont, *L'Afrique Etranglée*, Paris: Editions du Seuil, 1980. O'Brien, *The Political Economy of Underdevelopment*.

50. Gramsci, *Selections from the Prison Notebooks*, 177–178.

51. Hall, "Moving Right," 117.

52. *Afrique Contemporaine*, janvier–février 1981: 20–21.

53. Gellar, *Senegal*, 38, 118.

54. *Afrique Contemporaine*, mars–avril, 1981: 26–27.

55. *West Africa*, 19 January 1981: 102–104.

56. *West Africa*, 23 February 1981: 365.

57. Fall, *Sous-Développement et Démocratie Multipartisane*, 72–77.

58. *West Africa*, 25 January 1982: 213–217; 2 August 1982: 1984–1985; 21 February 1983: 460–461; *Jeune Afrique*, 19 janvier, 1983: 24–25.

59. *West Africa*, 2 August 1982: 1985.

60. *Jeune Afrique*, 19 janvier 1983: 24–25; *West Africa*, 21 February 1983: 460–461.

61. *West Africa*, 14 March 1983: 644–645.

62. *Takusaan*, 2 mars 1983: 2–15. *Le Soleil*, 2 mars 1983: 1–4.

63. Donal Cruise O'Brien, "Les Elections Sénégalaises du 27 février 1983," *Politique Africaine*, No. 11: 7–12; *West Africa*, 7 March 1983: 589–590.

64. *Takusaan*: 15.

65. O'Brien, "Les Elections Sénégalaises du 27 février 1983," 8 (my translation).

66. Donal Cruise O'Brien, "Senegal's Elections: What Went Wrong," *West Africa*, 21 March 1983: 714.

2

Democratization in Theoretical Perspective

In theory, the rise and breakdown of liberal democracy has been explained in a variety of ways. For the purposes of this study, it is only necessary to distinguish five main schools of thought: the African socialist, the liberal-developmentalist, the princely, the economy of affection, and the dependent-Marxian. A critical analysis of their fundamental assumptions will show their obdurate limitations in explaining the Senegalese road to liberal democracy. As a result, in the next chapter I will offer a different paradigm based on Gramsci's conception of passive revolution.

African Socialism

In the immediate aftermath of independence, Africans inherited westernized liberal systems of government that had little to do with their colonial experiences and their traditional customs and values. Not surprisingly, in an effort to accelerate the processes of decolonization and indigenization, Africans rejected the Western parliamentary model and developed their own conception of political representation and democracy. This conception was rooted in the ideal of the one-party state, which was hailed as embodying the collective harmony and unity of the African way of life. The one-party state was presented as the most effective means of promoting economic development, national reconstruction, and social equality. It was to express the specifically African conception of socialism, a socialism rooted in the heritage of precolonial communal values, modes of producing, and methods of working and sharing. In short, both African socialism and the one-party state were to replace the individualistic bourgeois ethos and the conflict-ridden politics of a foreign European model.

The one-party state, argued its defenders, expressed the African reality of classless and nonantagonistic social relations, the requirements of unity to wage the war against underdevelopment, and the imperative of staving off all forms of neocolonialism. As Kwame Nkrumah explained:

> We believe that a monolithic party is necessary in an excolonial state which is inevitably faced with the task of correcting past maladjustment, years of neglect and of colonial mental conditioning, and of building a new, really independent, happy and proud state. Such a young state cannot afford to dissipate its national efforts through the senseless wranglings and obstructive and destructive tactics that organized political opposition encourages. Besides, it is through such opposition parties that colonialism and imperialism seek to perpetuate their hold on the country.[1]

The supporters of African socialism described the suppression of organized opposition and the erection of a monolithic one-party state as not contradictory to the ideals of democracy, social justice, and popular participation; in the African context they were the sine qua non of such ideals. The democracy of African socialism was not a copy of the Anglo-Saxon two-party system; in fact, it was rooted in the precolonial African terrain.[2] This terrain was free from conflicts, individual and communal interests were never at war, and both the individual and the community were living in freedom and practicing democracy. Not surprisingly, this precolonial heritage imparted to Africa a classlessness that was further reinforced by the popular unity generated by the modern experience of nationalism. In these circumstances, the wishes of the community and, indeed, the practice of democracy itself were embodied in the single-party system. As Julius Nyerere put it: "[Where] there is one party, and that party is identified with the nation as a whole, the foundations of democracy are firmer than they can ever be where you have two or more parties, each representing only a section of the community."[3]

The one-party state symbolized the essence of democracy in the context of African socialism; it recaptured and modernized the precolonial culture system and, as such, it represented the

Africanization of democracy. The African one-party state, however, was not to be assimilated to its Communist counterpart. Whereas the latter's dogmatism and restricted membership implied that it would never "free itself from fear of overthrow by those it ... excluded," the former was a "national movement which [was opened] to all, which [was] identified with the whole nation, [and which therefore had] nothing to fear from the discontent of any excluded section of society, for there is then no such section of society...."[4]

This is not to say that disagreements were nonexistent or that they were not to be tolerated, for free debates are an essential precondition of democracy, but rather that policies and decisions ensuing from democratic practice were binding to all—even those who campaigned against them. In other words, democracy required also disciplined acceptance of political defeat.[5] Without it the goals of development would be elusive and indeed unreachable.

Such disciplined acceptance was grounded in the African way of life whose long discursive processes assured that decisions would be reached on a communal consensus. In the words of Senghor:

> Europeans, those of the East and those of the West, speak to us often of 'Democracy,' as if we didn't have our own conception which cedes nothing to that of Europe.
>
> African democracy is essentially founded on the *palabre*. The *palabre* is a dialogue, or better yet, a colloquium, where each has the right to speak, where everyone takes the floor to express his opinion. Formerly, even the dead were consulted. But once opinion was expressed, the minority followed the majority to manifest their unanimity. This unanimous opinion was then vigorously applied without deviation. The severe offender had to atone and seek expiation in order to reintroduce order into the community and universe. Otherwise, he was excluded. You can see this speaking democracy was as far from dictatorship as anarchy and laissez-faire. The problem now is to restore this democracy under a modern form.
>
> Another trap of Europe consists in persuading us that what is important is not the People, the Nation-State, but the individual, with his needs, passions, tastes, and fantasies. As if liberty was to be confounded with license, as if the individual could realize himself outside of the group, and the group outside of the Nation.[6]

With a silenced meaningful opposition, the masses could

express their voices only through the party. The party had to be supreme, it had to possess absolute authority because "it is the uniting force that guides and pilots the nation and is the nerve center of the positive operations in the struggle for African irredentism. Its supremacy cannot be challenged."[7] United in and educated by the party, the masses were supposed to create and erect the foundations of the state and the nation. The masses were the party and the party was the masses. As the embodiment of the nation and of all institutions, the party had to be the sole source of legitimacy; it had to be unique.

This quest for unanimity and for the higher collective good, as against the acceptance of conflict and individual as well as class interests, contained inevitably the germs of intolerance and repression. The single party became the unique voice of the people, and the unique voice became the exclusive voice of the ruling groups, and soon the voice of the ruling groups became the voice of a unique individual. The nation was the party but the party was the undisputed and unchallenged leader. Thus started the descent of the one-party state into the cruel hell of dictatorship, privilege, praetorianism, and injustice.

The glorious visions of accelerated economic development, social equality, democratic practice, and political harmony projected by the one-party state soon disintegrated. Consequently, the legitimacy of the party, as well as that of its leaders and organizations, collapsed under the weight of massive disaffection and alienation. As Claude Ake has argued:

> The one-party system eventually emerged as the classic form of the depoliticised African society. It allowed the ruling class to dispense with the substance of democratic participation while retaining its formal aspects. It is of course quite possible for democracy to be practised in the context of the one-party system. However, the experience of one-party systems in Africa does not demonstrate this possibility. The establishment of the one-party system in Africa involved the use of much coercion and even violence. It entailed one faction of the ruling class using coercion to make itself hegemonic, as well as using coercion to force the masses to acquiesce in the reduction of their political participation. And even after the establishment of the one-party system, the use of force continued to be necessary because the contradictions within the ruling class and the contradictions between the ruling class and the masses were so great that a one-party system which was so totally at odds with this reality

could only be maintained by force.[8]

The one-party state was not just repressive, it failed miserably in the task that it had set for itself. Instead of inducing unity and harmony, it generated ethnic favoritism and divisions; instead of promoting economic development, it fostered material stagnation and decline; instead of ushering in social equality, it led to corruption and inequalities; and, instead of establishing a viable political order, it engendered fissiparous tendencies, military coups, and civil wars.[9] Moreover, the one-party state was never capable of establishing its control over the vast majority of the population; it never effectively reached the peasantry to integrate it in successful processes of mobilization and participation. It lacked the resources, legitimacy, and organizational skills.[10] It soon developed into an urban phenomenon bent exclusively on maintaining the privileges and interests of the ruling groups; and this it could not even do successfully as the history of military coups attests. Thus, the one-party state proved to be neither a necessary prerequisite nor an effective instrument for political and economic development. In fact, it may have been a serious hindrance to such development.

In spite of the failure of the African one-party state, most ruling classes have tended to cling desperately to it as their preferred mode of governance. Staying in power being their overriding interest and goal, and still believing that the maintenance of stability is best guaranteed by the creation and consolidation of organizational juggernauts, the ruling classes have persisted in their efforts to build one-party systems. But it is not preordained that they must do so, nor that they are incapable of setting up different institutional arrangements that would be more democratic and better equipped to obtain greater legitimacy and popular compliance. Indeed, as we shall see in the following chapters, the Senegalese ruling class, headed by Senghor and then Diouf, gradually came to understand that its survival required the ushering in of more liberal political structures. These structures ultimately crystallized in the creation of a multiparty bourgeois democracy.

The assumptions behind the growth of the one-party system have not only been invalidated by the very practical experience of this system, but they have also been rejected by some of its most fervent adherents, as the case of Senghor exemplifies. Indeed, the Senegalese ruling class has come to accept Jacques

Mariel Nzouankeu's arguments for liberal democracy:

> For a long time it was thought and taught that democratic pluralism ... could only exist in the economically advanced nations: that liberal democracy was a luxury for underdeveloped countries, notably African ones. The arguments that were put forward to support this autocratic thesis have not varied: political pluralism undermines the unity of action required for development; in new nations, political pluralism threatens to unleash centrifugal forces and thus secessions; political pluralism generates a typically Western model of society unsuited to African conditions.
>
> For several years, these myths have failed to correspond to reality. We know indeed that there is no necessary correlation between a country's level of economic development and its form of government.... The level of economic development does not determine the viability of political pluralism.
>
> [The Senegalese model confirms] the fact that pluralism is not only compatible with underdevelopment, but that it also constitutes the fundamental condition for development and national unity.[11]

While Nzouankeu is probably right in his assertions, their triumphant tone should invite caution and scepticism. Indeed, as we further examine it, we shall see that Senegalese democracy suffers from clear limitations to its liberalism and, as with all bourgeois forms of representation, it is replete with contradictions and constraints. Moreover, the backward, dependent, and peripheral character of its economy can only contribute to exacerbating these contradictions and constraints. In this vein, it is wrong to dismiss the crucial importance of material structures in the ushering in of bourgeois liberal democracies; historically, the viability of such democracies has heavily depended on the elasticity and expansive capacity of capitalism. This is not to say that the development of capitalism engenders liberal democracy. On the contrary, as we shall argue in the following section on the liberal-developmentalist school, there is no necessary and logical linkage between capitalism and democracy; the most that can be safely advanced is that the contradictions unleashed by capitalism may open serious cracks in the wall of bourgeois domination from which may flow democratic practices and reforms.[12]

Liberal Developmentalism

The liberal-developmentalist theory claims that there is a positive association between capitalist industrialization and democracy and that the latter is a necessary consequence of the former. In other words, capitalist industrialization that destroys the archaic subsistence economy, as well as the immemorial practices and superstitions of traditional society, pushes to the fore the impersonal and secular cash nexus of the market and the rational spirit of scientific bourgeois culture. In these circumstances, the population becomes educated and well-off and, as such, it demands and obtains democratic rule. Simply put, for the liberal-developmentalist school, democracy equals capitalist industrialization and modernity.[13] In addition, this school portrays both capitalist industrialization and modernity as the only logical and rational culmination of the process of development itself. It assumes that social change transforms undifferentiated and traditional societies into economic and political systems comparable to those that emerged from the industrialization of Western Europe and North America. The industrialization of the underdeveloped nations in this perspective must necessarily follow a direction analogous to that of its Western counterparts. An ideal type of developed society is thus derived from the "Western complex system" and juxtaposed against those underdeveloped traditional societies, which are supposed to move inevitably towards this ideal type if they are to industrialize. This movement along a continuum between tradition and modernity is established as a measuring rod determining the progress of a particular social unit. Those communities that have already experienced a specifically capitalist form of industrialization are seen as presaging the future direction of social change in underdeveloped nations.

The problem with the developmentalist theory is not so much its idealized and selective construct of Western societies, which ignores phenomena such as Nazi Germany, nor the persistence of traditional norms and values in the most advanced capitalist societies. Neither is it the neglect of the adaptive capacities of traditional man to modernity and change. Rather, the central problem is its ex post facto explanation of industrialization and democratization. Far from being an explanatory framework of development, the developmentalist theory is instead a generalized and often mythical description of the democratic impact of capitalism on already industrialized nations. Substituting description for explanation, the developmentalist theory has little to offer in the elucidation of the process of change in modernizing societies. The only conclusion that can be drawn from it is the tautological thesis that to become modern and democratic is to cease to be traditional and autocratic. In other words, although the transition from tradition to modernity is said to entail the attainment of a particular end-state whose hallmark is a capitalist economy and a bourgeois democracy, there is little analysis of the causes and determinants of this transition. Apart from its concept of Western cultural and technological diffusion, the developmentalist theory has a teleological explanation of social change, which is described as being caused by the mysterious needs and functional requirements of the system.

How these needs and functional requirements are generated, and why they should be similar to those of advanced capitalist societies are questions that remain unanswered. Hence, to explain modernization by asserting that highly differentiated structures exist in order to sustain industrialization and that the market economy is the sine qua non of material growth and democracy is to use the consequences of Western development as universal causalities of development and democratization. The result of deriving explanations from the specifically capitalist and Western end-state is to neglect the diversity of history and the specificities of particular situations. It is to impose rigid parameters on the future of non-Western communities and to deny them the alternative of different choices and directions in their distinct historical environments.

Be that as it may, the developmentalist school believes that there is a compulsory and necessary association between capitalist economic structures and democratic regimes because democracies of the pluralistc type gradually emerged from the wombs of Western capitalist development. This assumption is based on the conviction that the expansive capacities of industrial capitalism not only generate the popular demand for democracy, but make democracy itself possible. Seymour Martin Lipset has defended this thesis in the following terms:

> Democracy is related to the state of economic development. The more well-to-do a nation, the greater the chances that it will sustain democracy. From Aristotle down to the present, men

have argued that only in a wealthy society in which relatively few citizens lived at the level of real poverty could there be a situation in which the mass of the population intelligently participate in politics and develop the self-restraint necessary to avoid succumbing to the appeals of irresponsible demagogues. A society divided between a large impoverished mass and a small favored elite results either in oligarchy [dictatorial rule of the small upper stratum] or in tyranny [popular-based dictatorship]. To give these two political forms modern labels, tyranny's face today is communism or Peronism; while oligarchy appears in the traditionalist dictatorships found in parts of Latin America, Thailand, Spain, or Portugal.[14]

It is true that the expansive capacity of wealthy capitalist societies is significant insofar as it provides to the ruling classes the material means with which they can maneuver the democratization of their mode of governance. But it is not in itself conducive to such democratization; democratization requires a certain degree of disunity in the ranks of the ruling classes, a disunity which opens certain cracks in the wall of domination and hence the possibility of successful reforms. In this respect, the social relations of capitalism tend to enhance the development of such disunity as they "create an internally competing, peacefully disunited ruling class.... divided into several fractions: mercantile, banking, industrial, agrarian, small and big."[15]   Although these divisions should not be exaggerated, because they quickly vanish in periods of acute crisis, they are significant in periods of normalcy.   They provide to the subordinate classes a certain political space in which they can operate reforming alliances with rival factions of the ruling classes.

These reforming alliances, however, are not the most important factor of democratization. The integration of the subordinate classes into a more liberal political framework is, above all, the result of popular struggles against the exclusive power of the dominant groups.   Hence, the history of democratization is the history of the class struggle. But, while ruling class concessions are the product of the conditions created by this struggle, they tend to crystallize only in the period ensuing after the successful containment of this very struggle.   In other words, ruling classes always resist the popular demands for reforms in the heat of confrontation, because they seek to demonstrate that they and only they can usher in, control, and guide the processes of democratization. In their eyes, to do otherwise would be to submit to irresponsible blackmail and to abdicate their very status.

The leadership of the ruling class in the process of democratization has consequences of vital importance for the shape and content of the new forms of popular participation and representation. Goran Therborn explains that

> the working-class movement was nowhere capable of achieving democracy by its own unaided resources.... Only in conjunction with external allies were the non-propertied masses able to gain democratic rights; and it was above all the propertied minorities who in the end answered the critical questions of timing and form—of when and how democracy was to be introduced. Thus, the process of democratization unfolded within the framework of the capitalist state, congealing in the form of bourgeois democracy rather than opening the road to popular revolution and socialist transformation.... Bourgeois democracy has always and everywhere been established in struggle against ... the bourgeoisie, but through political means and channels provided for by the capitalist state.... Thus, although bourgeois democracy is democratic government plus the rule of capital, its democratic component has been achieved and defended against the bourgeoisie.[16]

In this perspective, it is not economic wealth as such that provides the impetus for democratization, but popular struggles against bourgeois dominance. What wealth does, however, is to facilitate the making of ruling class concessions; it is not a necessary prerequisite for the establishment of bourgeois democracy. The most that historical experience allows us to say with any confidence is that capitalism generates basic contradictions between labor and capital from which democracy may spring. In other words, democracy has never developed as a spontaneous outgrowth of capitalist industrialization; on the contrary, it emerged as a result of popular struggles against bourgeois power.

Thus, the explanation of democratization given by the developmentalist school tends to be simplistic as it originates from a remorseless and unilateral stress on anglocentric historical experiences.[17] Moreover, it is clearly contradicted by the Senegalese case. Indeed, the rise of democracy in Senegal has corresponded with a profound economic crisis and has taken place in a non-industrialized peasant society. Both the absence of material abundance and the presence of Islam as a pervasive "unscientific" and traditional ethos have not prevented the ushering in of liberal democracy. Thus, the developmentalist paradigm is of little use in explaining the making of the Senegalese bourgeois-liberal regime.

It is also clear that Samuel Huntington's model of political decay, which reversed the analytical sequences of the developmentalist school, fails to elucidate the Senegalese phenomenon.[18] For Huntington the accelerated pace of modernization in the Third World leads to chaos and instability instead of democratic practice. That is, in the non-Western world there is a general crisis of governance expressed in the rise of praetorianism and authoritarianism because the "problems of the centralization of authority, national integration, social mobilization, economic development, political participation, social welfare have arisen not sequentially but simultaneously."[19] Therefore, for Huntington, democracy is unlikely to crystallize in the modernizing Third World. In a similar vein, Michael Lofchie has explained the decomposition and decay of African democracy:

The sequential pattern of crisis confrontation distinguishes Western historical experience markedly from that in Africa and other developing areas. One common feature of newly independent African states is that they must confront all these crises at once; that is, they must establish a unified sense of national identity, work out mutually agreeable constitutional arrangements, incorporate culturally diverse elements into the political system, and conduct extensive welfare programs simultaneously. In a political context in which the 'rules of the game' lack widespread consensual validity but universal suffrage encourages maximum popular involvement in the political process, the difficulties of formulating widely agreeable welfare policies are greater than representative systems can easily endure.
.... When representative structures have become so weakened or ineffectual ... a political vacuum is created which must be filled by an alternative source of leadership.... Where this has occurred, the most common leadership pattern is a personalistic cabinet autocracy, with a more or less fictional party organization performing a weak legitimization function.... In this situation, the very concept of representative government becomes discredited, and the regime loses the necessary support and legitimacy to remain in power. When this occurs, the military is likely to seize control and as an

instrument of national purification will usually be able to attract
popular support for a period of military rule.[20]

Such a conclusion, however valid for most African political
systems, clearly defies the Senegalese experience whose process
of democratization was a direct response to the massive
pressures of modernization itself.

In an attempt to explain the theoretical discrepancies of the
developmentalist school, Robert Jackson and Carl Rosberg[21]
have revived the old personalist paradigm according to which it
is leadership which determines politics rather than
socioeconomic structures and processes.[22] Their adaptation of
this old paradigm to the African specificity can be called the
"princely" explanation of democracy.

Political Leadership and Princely Rule

Jackson and Rosberg have argued that in Africa the absence of
clear institutional frameworks of universally accepted rules of
political conduct has contributed to the rise of personal rule. In
other words, it is leadership and the quality of this leadership
that determine the nature of African politics.[23]

The character of personal rule is decisive in the making of
African politics. Jackson and Rosberg distinguish four main
types of personal rule: princely, autocratic, prophetic and
tyrannical.[24] Although all four reflect a "dynamic world of
political will and action that is ordered less by institutions than
by personal authorities and power," they differ in the scope and
severity of their rule and the vision and nature of their
ideologies.[25] For our purposes, however, the discussion will be
limited to princely rule because Jackson and Rosberg claimed
with justification that President Senghor was the African prince
par excellence.[26] In other words, Senghor had mastered the art
of what he himself termed "politician politics."[27] This politics
is the "race for preferments," and it is the essence of princely
rule. "To rule as a Prince is to preside over the struggle for
preferments, to encourage it, to recognize that it is a source of the
ruler's and the regime's legitimacy, but not to allow it to get out
of hand, nor to let any leader emerge as a serious challenger."[28]

For Rosberg and Jackson, Senghor's mastery of princely
rule was the determining factor of Senegalese politics; in fact,

the rise of Senghorian guided democracy was an expression of its partial institutionalization and, thus, of its success in creating universally accepted rules of political conduct. Such institutionalization was facilitated by the norms and rules guiding the relationships existing between the prince and the different factions of the ruling class. These relationships, being based on private agreements and understandings that were mutually respected by both, contained the seeds of formal constitutional arrangements. As Rosberg and Jackson point out:

> It is this incipient constitutionalism of princely rule—his emphasis on agreements, understandings, and promises —which suggests that it is long-standing princely regimes, more than any of the other forms of personal rule, that have the best chance to become institutionalized, for the private compacts between ruler and oligarchs can become the foundation of an institutional principle of government if the ruling class is prepared to accept them as such, and if these compacts can gain legitimacy from the larger society.[29]

Moreover, the prince and, in particular, his followers have a vested interest in the routinization and rationalization of princely rule itself. The charismatic attributes that the prince acquired as a result of his leading role in the struggle for independence have to be institutionalized if political stability is to be maintained, and if the material privileges and ideological supremacy of his "community of disciples" are to be preserved. Max Weber remarks that

> charismatic authority may be said to exist only *in statu nascendi.* It cannot remain stable, but becomes either traditionalized or rationalized, or a combination of both.
> The following are the principal motives underlying this transformation: (a) The ideal and also the material interests of the followers in the continuation and continual reactivation of the community, (b) the still stronger ideal and also stronger material interests of the members of the administrative staff, the disciples, the party workers, or others in continuing their relationship. Not only this, but they have an interest in continuing it in such a way that both from an ideal and a material point of view, their own position is put on a stable everyday basis.[30]

Paradoxically, then, the success of princely rule may

ultimately imply the institutionalization of politics and consequently the abolition of princely rule itself. This paradox describes well the Senegalese experiment in building democracy. Indeed, the peaceful departure of the prince (Senghor) was possible precisely because he had sufficiently institutionalized the framework of Senegalese politics. That such institutionalization was ultimately completed under Diouf is a tribute to the princely qualities of Diouf himself.

Thus, Jackson and Rosberg's concept of personal rule is a useful heuristic guide in elucidating the rise of Senegalese democracy. Yet the primacy that it attributes to personality and individual talent in masterminding the political process is exaggerated and simplistic; it underestimates the significance of broader economic and social structures in the making of social change. In short, it fails to take notice of Marx's injunction that "[People] make their own history, but they do not make it just as they please; they do not make it under circumstances chosen by themselves, but under circumstances directly found, given and transmitted from the past."[31]

These circumstances that form the existing structures of society represent the explanatory basis of both the mode of production and the dependent-Marxian paradigms.

The Economy of Affection and the "Soft State"

The concept of the "peasant mode of production" implies the existence of a separate material and institutional structure—the "economy of affection"—which operates as an alternative "space" to the dominant state system.[32] In other words, this alternative space allows the peasantry to "exit" the demands and policies formulated by central political authorities.[33] The "economy of affection," which "denotes a network of support, communications and interaction among structurally defined groups connected by blood, kin, community or other affinities ..." has an autonomy of its own and thus it can successfully resist integration into the prevailing macroeconomy.[34]

Such resistance stems from the peasants' capacity to exist as independent producers who have yet to be "captured" by the state system and by the dominant classes. Goran Hyden argues:

> As the productive and reproductive needs of the peasants can be met without the support of other social classes, relations between

those who rule and those who till the land are not firmly rooted in
the production system as such. Instead, appropriations by those
in control of the state are made in the form of taxation and as
such they are simple deductions from an already produced stock
of values. These are tributary rather than productive relations
and they do imply a much more limited degree of social control.
In this respect, African countries are societies without a state.
The latter sits suspended in 'mid-air' over society and is not an
integral mechanism of the day-to-day productive activities of
society....

Because the state is structurally superfluous from the point
of view of the individual producer, it is not difficult to see that the
peasant experiences any public policy aimed at improving his
agriculture as a 'foreign' intervention. Because he owns the land,
or at least has the undisputed right to till it, his ability to escape
such policy demands is much greater than that of a tenant under
feudal rule or a worker under capitalism.[35]

Therefore, the state is seen as being incapable of sustaining
and reproducing existing social relations and, specifically, of
controlling the labor force in the interest of any program of
economic growth. Suspended in mid-air without roots in a
strong indigenous bourgeoisie and without the power to enforce
the systemic and authoritative allocation of values, the state is
"soft" and impotent. As a result, the vast majority of the
population—the peasantry—has the option of rejecting its
integration in the state system, and it remains "uncaptured."
Precisely because it can choose to remain uncaptured it promotes
the continued survival of the economy of affection as an
alternative mode of production to the macroeconomic program of
the state. The peasant mode of production therefore challenges
and erodes the implantation of modern industrial structures
and sustains traditional economic methods and ideologies. In
this respect, the softness of the state represents an obdurate
constraint on the overall development of African societies. No
social class is powerful enough to impose its hegemony and
construct an effective and productive economic system.

In this view, African politics are a politics without ruling
classes. Hyden contends:

The dilemma facing African leaders is that because the state is
not structurally tied to society they are not in a position to
exercise systemic power. They lack the more subtle institutional
means that are at the disposal of a government in

societies where the state is firmly rooted in the productive system of the country and where, therefore, it can be used to shape the system at large. Seen in this perspective, the image of the African leader as being extremely powerful is mistaken.... In this respect, it is difficult to call the African holding state power a 'ruling class.' They are not the carriers of a hegemonic 'bourgeois' culture and prefer to act as patrons of their respective home communities.[36]

The absence of institutionalized power, however, does not preclude the existence of authoritarianism, dictatorial rule, and tyranny. Paradoxically, the soft state creates the perfect terrain for these arbitrary and violent forms of governance. As Hyden himself recognized: "The fact that the state is still not structurally rooted in the prevailing systems of peasant production in Africa invites authoritarianism and often arbitrariness in political decisions."[37]

The question this inevitably implies is why and how can the state unleash its arbitrary violence, particularly against the lower and working strata of the population, if it stands in mid-air, uncontrolled by any ruling class? Hence, the important issue is not whether the state is soft, but whether it is soft for, or harsh against, particular groups and classes. In short, whose benefits are best served by the softness of the state? It is true that in most African countries social discipline is weak and power lacks institutionalization, but this general systemic weakness favors in disproportionate ways the interests of the privileged ruling circles, according to Gunnar Myrdal. Myrdal writes:

> The laxity and arbitrariness in a national community that can be characterized as a soft state can be, and are, exploited for personal gain by people who have economic, social, and political power.... When policy measures have been instituted specifically aimed at ameliorating conditions for the lower strata, they have either not been implemented and enforced or have been distorted so as to favor the not-so-poor and to discriminate against the masses.[38]

The soft state is neither neutral nor in mid-air. The unleashing of state power, often expressed in violent repression, serves the interests of the dominant faction of the ruling class. It depoliticizes the subaltern groups by eliminating their independent organs of representation and by reducing their participation in decision making. The emergence of the one party state throughout Africa is the means to these ends. In addition, the one-party state is the vehicle through which material resources are acquired and distributed since the state in Africa is the fundamental agent of capital accumulation and extraction. In these circumstances, it is not surprising that the struggle for controlling the state, in conditions of monolithic political structures and generalized material scarcity, becomes Hobbesian, violent, and deadly.

Such a situation of political insecurity has transformed the one-party state into a system breeding disorder rather than order. This, in turn, has generated a process of escalating repression as those ruling the state have sought to maintain and preserve their absolute monopoly of power. As Claude Ake states:

> The threat of political instability engendered by pent-up resentment has not given the ruling class the confidence and security to practise democracy. The repression needed to establish and maintain the single-party system aided the development of the contradictions in society. Repression and the monopoly of political power increased the premium on the attainment of political power. The premium was already very high because of the use of political power to create an economic base and its use for the accumulation of capital. The premium on political power now became singularly high because political power had to be captured not only as a necessary condition for economic welfare but also as a necessary condition for avoiding brutalisation if not extermination.[39]

Political instability in Africa is, therefore, rooted more in the extreme politicization of the state as an organ to be monopolized for absolute power and accelerated economic advancement than in the softness of the state, as Hyden would have it. To characterize the state as being soft is to miss the class relationships and class struggles that provide the social context that molds and shapes the state itself. Thus, if the state in Africa is relatively weak in terms of its capacity to impose its authority on all sectors of society, it is nonetheless powerful enough to unleash its violence against particular groups and classes. The relative impotence of the state to enforce its own rules is biased impotence; it is an impotence that consistently favors and enhances the power, interests, and status of the well-off and privileged classes. Paul Harrison explains:

The state ... is not uniformly soft. It would be more accurate to
describe it as a soft-centred state with an extremely hard exterior:
soft to the privileged, hard to the poor, a sort of dictatorship of the
elite over the poor masses, while the rich are left to get away,
often literally, with murder.[40]

In this instance, it is significant to note the tolerance of the
state toward the illegal acquisition and reproduction of wealth
through the rapidly expanding black markets of Africa.   The
phenomenon of the black market economy, known as the
magendo in East Africa and the *kalabule* in Ghana, indicates
that the softness of the state is more a symptom of ruling class
interests than institutional weakness and fragility.[41]   The
magendo persists because it serves the material and political
purposes of the ruling class. It constitutes a source of wealth and
a means of ascending to membership in the ruling class.
Accordingly, the *magendo*, in spite of its autonomy from the
formal structures of state power, depends inevitably on the power
holders for its continued survival and expansion. The state will
not close down the *magendo* operations, because they are too
profitable for both state agents and *magendo* entrepreneurs.   In
his study of Uganda, Nelson Kasfir remarks that

neither the Amin nor the interim post-liberation governments
acted to plug [*magendo*] loopholes, presumably because civil
servants from top to bottom were highly conscious of their
vested interest in permitting the state to maintain them. As
magendo operators moved into legitimate economic sectors, their
involvement with state officials would necessarily have had to
grow more extensive. The operation of *magendo* in Uganda was
significantly dependent on and continued to be related to the
state.[42]

In contrast to this symbiotic relationship between state and
magendo, the state-peasant relationship in spite of the peasant's
capacity to exit has been characterized by domination and
subordination. The fact that peasants enjoy certain means of
exit from governmental policies should not conceal the negative
and pervasive impact of the state on their livelihood and mode of
production.   The peasants' exit is a choice of last resort
reflecting their desire to avoid the adverse effects of official
policies. It is not an indication of the peasants' victorious
independence from state interference. The peasants withdraw
from the public realm precisely because of the harshness of state

decisions. Thus, the exit of the peasantry is more a symptom of the hard-centered nature of the state than of its softness.[43] Robert Bates argues that

> the peasants dodge and maneuver to avoid the deprivations inflicted upon them by public policy. They use the market against the state.
>
> But this ... should not be heralded as a triumph for the peasantry. The fact is that the peasants avoid the state by taking refuge in alternatives that are clearly second best. They move out of the production of the crops that are most profitable and into economic activities that have become more profitable only because they are less heavily taxed. In thus changing the way they employ their resources, they incur economic losses.[44]

In this sense, while the state may be soft insofar as it is incapable of both enforcing the totality of its authority on all sectors of society and penetrating effectively all the realms of social activity, it is not uniformly soft in its impact on the different social classes. The concept of the soft state is therefore misleading because it masks the authoritarian character of most African states and the uneven and biased impact of state intervention.   In this instance, it is preferable to allude to Gramsci's notion of the "integral" state, a state that crystallizes the historical unity of the ruling classes, as well as the "organic relations between ... political society and 'civil society.'"[45] The integral state expresses, therefore, the effective hegemonic capacity and repressive potential that the ruling class exercises over civil society and political society respectively.

> [There are] two major superstructural 'levels': the one that can be called 'civil society,' that is the ensemble of organisms commonly called 'private,' and that of 'political society' or 'the state.' These two levels correspond on the one hand to the function of 'hegemony' which the dominant group exercises throughout society and on the other hand to that of 'direct domination' or command exercised through the State and 'juridical' government.   The functions in questions are precisely organisational and connective.[46]

In Africa, the absence of a hegemonic ruling class has resulted in the persistent use of the coercive powers of the state. This absence stems from the incapacity of the ruling classes in obtaining the "spontaneous" consent of the masses to the general direction they wish to impose on society. In these circumstances, social discipline and order are imposed by direct domination on those who do not consent either actively or passively to the rule of the governing classes. The necessity of direct domination is an indication that the state has yet to become integral and that it has yet to realize the organic unity between hegemony and force. Whereas the state cannot effectively expand the domain of its authority to obtain the obedience of all its subjects, it has, however, the capacity to crush fundamental political challenges. The state may lack the power to eliminate all existing means of "exit," but it possesses sufficient coercive might to repress serious contending and opposing "voices."[47] In fact, the means of exit represent a safety valve for the continued survival of most African political systems. Exit embodies the safest and most profitable expression of discontent, as the popular articulation of voices is much too costly and dangerous in the African context of authoritarian one-party states.

It is true, however, that certain degrees of exit or voice may precipitate the collapse of the state as an institution. As Albert O. Hirschman puts it:

> Every state—and indeed every organization—requires for its establishment and existence some limitations or ceilings on the extent of exit or of voice or of both. In other words, there are levels of exit [disintegration] and voice [disruption] beyond which it is impossible for an organization to exist as an organization. At the same time, an organization needs minimal or floor levels of exit and voice in order to receive the necessary feedback about its performance. Every organization thus navigates between the Scylla of disintegration-disruption and the Charybdis of deterioration due to lack of feedback.[48]

In Africa, most ruling classes have restricted so stringently the level of voice that the masses have found in exit the only means of expressing their opposition without risking the brutal suffering of state repression. Hence, it is the incapacity of the ruling classes to tolerate and institutionalize a relatively high level of voice that has, paradoxically, contributed to the development and persistence of exit. Such an incapacity indicates the ruling classes' failure to control, shape, and guide political participation; it is symptomatic of their non-hegemonic status.

In general, African ruling classes have been unable to impose their "intellectual and moral leadership"; they have been besieged by a continuous and persistent "crisis of authority."[49] Their reliance on coercion alone is the manifestation of their incapacity to obtain popular compliance to their authority. They lack the necessary legitimacy to establish an integral state which can command without the pervasive use of force. As Max Weber explains, the existence and continued functionning of a political regime requires more than the exclusive capacity to repress:

> Every genuine form of domination implies a minimum of voluntary compliance, that is, an interest (based on ulterior motives or genuine acceptance) in obedience.
> Not every case of domination makes use of economic means; still less does it always have economic objectives....The basis of every authority, and correspondingly of every kind of willingness to obey, is a belief, a belief by virtue of which persons exercising authority are lent prestige. The composition of this belief is seldom altogether simple.[50]

In Africa, however, the virtual absence of such a belief has stemmed from the ruling classes' peripheral and weak position in the world of production. This is not at all to say that African ruling classes have not attempted to construct an ideological system legitimizing their rule; in fact, they have been engaged in a persistent attempt to build such a system, but they have failed rather miserably.[51] The stagnating, declining, and dependent nature of most African economies has imposed obdurate limitations on the hegemonic capacities of these ruling classes. This has resulted in the emergence of authoritarian and dictatorial regimes. As the next chapters will attempt to demonstrate, the case of Senegal invalidates such a general conclusion. Facing a systemic crisis, the Senegalese ruling class has sought to establish its hegemony through a passive revolution rooted in democratization rather than repression. It has done so in a context of acute economic problems, increasing popular mobilization, and social dislocation. Hence, the rise of authoritarian regimes should not be unilaterally linked to the material structures characterizing the underdeveloped nations of the capitalist "periphery" as the dependent-Marxian paradigm would have it. The next section is a critical analysis of this paradigm.

The Dependent-Marxian Paradigm

For the dependent-Marxian school, the Third World or the "periphery" of the international capitalist system cannot create liberal forms of bourgeois democracy similar to those of the industrialized "center."[52] The dependent nature of "peripheral capitalism" imposes inflexible limits to democratic rule; in fact, it requires the institutionalization of dictatorship and repression. In other words, the insertion of the periphery into the world capitalist system implies its exploitation by the center and its incapacity to generate a sustaining self-reliant economy.[53] This incapacity is embedded in the nature of peripheral capitalism whose external orientation creates massive contradictions between domestic needs and domestic production.[54]

Production is geared toward exports and the privileged and limited market of the domestic ruling class. The requirements of such production imply, therefore, the "superexploitation" of "peripheral labor"[55] and the repressive means that this superexploitation entails.[56] In short, peripheral capitalism is incapable of creating mass markets because its very survival hinges upon the persistence of cheap wages. This reality, in turn, creates the terrain for repressive political regimes rather than liberal forms of bourgeois democracy.

Moreover, the peripheral state[57] represents more the interests of the bourgeoisies of the center than those of the dependent and weak peripheral ruling classes.[58] Thus, for some advocates of the dependent-Marxian school it is the unequal international division of labor and the requirements of capitalist accumulation that are the decisive determinants of the peripheral state.[59] As André Gunder Frank puts it:

> In the dependent economies of the Third World the dependent state is ... an essential instrument for the administration of the dependent role of the Third World economies in the international division of labor and the capitalist world process of capital accumulation. Increasingly also, the Third World state mediates between its national capital—and labor—and international capital; and as a dependent state it does so substantially to the benefit of international capital at the relative cost to national capital and at the absolute sacrifice of local labor.[60]

Not surprisingly, this "absolute sacrifice of local labor" engenders a general social crisis that can only be "resolved" through the "institutionalization of political repression and often the militarization of society."[61]

The material and social basis of peripheral capitalist nations impels the ruling class to adopt stringent and authoritarian measures against the demands and aspirations of the popular classes. Workers and peasants are to be forced into compliance with the severe requirements of capital accumulation and profitability. They are brutally forced to put up with the adverse impact of low wages, social dislocation, and declining living standards. Clive Thomas explains the crystallization of the authoritarian state as follows:

> The ability to maintain existing patterns of internal domination rests heavily on the ability of the state to win a reduction in the growth of real wages and the standard of living of the masses, along with increased worker productivity. Without these there can be no lasting increase in the profitability of the state and private sectors.... It is out of the effort to ensure increased profits and a reduced share of wages that the state is forced to restructure, and it is out of this process that an authoritarian state emerges. In other words, the crisis of the society and the world economy together engender a crisis that threatens the continuation of the regime in power, as well as the continued social and economic domination of the class and state on whose behalf it rules. It is because of this that the authoritarian state is the specific product of a conjuncture of world capitalism and peripheral capitalist development. Its imposition is the ruling-class response to the crisis confronting the society.[62]

Thus, what is crucial to this type of dependent-Marxian analysis is not so much the internal dimensions of the crisis but rather its externality and alien causes. It is the peripheralism of underdeveloped nations generated by imperialism that inevitably constrains the ruling classes to opt for authoritarianism.

This unilateral stress on the external aspects of peripheral capitalism has provoked an analytical reaction that has reasserted the primacy or equality of domestic factors in determining the politics of dependent societies.[63] Although this new analysis acknowledges the significance of dependence, it does so only in the context of the domestic class struggle. In other words, imperialism imposes the domination of foreign interests on the Third World, not necessarily because they are foreign, but rather because these interests just happen to correspond to those of the ruling peripheral bourgeoisies.[64] These bourgeoisies have a relative autonomy from the structural requirements of international capitalism even if they are constrained by these powerful structures. Such relative autonomy, however, does not abolish the necessity of repression; in fact, the domestic class struggle and the necessity of capitalist accumulation find their ultimate expression in the rise of bureaucratic authoritarianism. The "bureaucratic authoritarian state," in the words of O'Donnell, represents "first and foremost, [the] guarantor and organizer of the domination exercised through a class structure subordinated to the upper fractions of a highly oligopolized and transnationalized bourgeoisie."[65]

Thus, bureaucratic authoritarianism is a coercive, exclusionary, "depoliticizing," and anti-popular system responding almost exclusively to the interests of the transnationalized upper bourgeoisie. The emergence of the bureaucratic authoritarian state reflects not merely the political crisis whereby the demands and the threat posed by proletarian and peasant classes are repressively suppressed by the privileged groups;[66] it also symbolizes the coercive resolution of a particular stage in the history of capital accumulation in the periphery.[67] Put another way, the exit from the impasse created by the import-substitution process leads to the adoption of a strategy bent on "deepening" industrialization through an "open door" policy toward foreign capital and on reducing popular consumption and wages.[68] This inevitably involves the denationalization of the peripheral economy and the imposition of austerity on an already destitute working class. Both processes require, in turn, the institutionalization of authoritarianism and the depoliticization of the masses.

Therefore, whether dependent-Marxian scholars emphasize the primacy of the world capitalist system or that of the domestic class struggle in determining the nature of the peripheral state, they all agree that this state can only be authoritarian. In short, the peripheral state depoliticizes the masses and renders them politically impotent; and depoliticization expresses the ascendancy of the repressive apparatus of the state and thus the rule of the "specialists of coercion." In the African context, it has entailed the consolidation of what Ake has called "political monoliths" whereby "every regime assumes its exclusive right to rule and prohibits organized opposition." Furthermore, adds Ake, "depoliticization has made ... African politics particularly brutal."[69]

Now, while it is clear that the periphery in general and Africa in particular conform to the overall diagnostic of the dependent-Marxian school, Senegal departs from it in significant and fundamental ways. Indeed, Senegal is a dependent monocrop society whose economy is profoundly shaped by the vagaries of the international market and the process of capitalist accumulation on a world scale.[70] As such, it has faced the familiar problems associated with the vicissitudes of industrialization through import-substitution.[71] Also, the Senegalese bourgeoisie is extremely weak and it has had to coexist with a financially powerful expatriate community of French and Lebanese entrepreneurs.[72] Still, the economic crisis generated by these patterns of dependence has led to liberalization and politicization rather than brutal repression and massive alienation. As the Senegalese case demonstrates, democratization and liberal forms of representation are compatible with the rule of a weak, embryonic, and dependent bourgeoisie.

Conclusion

In this chapter, I examined different and competing theories of democratization and argued that none of them was able to comprehend adequately the conditions and processes conducive to the liberalization of a peripheral society like Senegal. While the African socialist and princely paradigms suffered from a political and cultural determinism that largely ignored the material realities constraining and affecting African society, the liberal developmentalist, economy of affection, and dependent-Marxian conceptualizations failed to consider seriously the fundamental realm of statecraft in the construction and reconstruction of liberal modes of governance because of their economic determinism. By unilaterally stressing a particular level of analysis each theory became one-dimensional and was incapable of apprehending the totality of the historical process. This is not to say that the theories presented in this chapter have no validity, but rather that by themselves they cannot elucidate the Senegalese political transformation. Clearly, then, what is required is a paradigm that integrates certain elements of these theories into a new and more comprehensive explanatory framework. The next chapters are an attempt to construct such a framework.

Notes

1. As quoted in Aristide R. Zolberg, *Creating Political Order*, Chicago: Rand McNally, 1966, 58.
2. Julius Nyerere, *Freedom and Unity*, Dar Es Salaam: Oxford University Press, 1967, 105–106.
3. Ibid., 196.
4. Ibid., 201.
5. Julius Nyerere, *Freedom and Development*, New York: Oxford University Press, 1973, 63.
6. As quoted in Irving Leonard Markovitz, *Léopold Sédar Senghor and the Politics of Négritude*, New York: Atheneum, 1969, 195–196.
7. Kwame Nkrumah, *I Speak of Freedom: A Statement of African Ideology*, New York: Praeger, 1961, 209.
8. Claude Ake, *A Political Economy of Africa*, New York: Longman, 1981, 181.
9. Rupert Emerson, "The Prospects for Democracy in Africa," in Michael F. Lofchie, ed., *The State of the Nations* , Berkeley: University of California Press, 1971, 239–257. Immanuel Wallerstein, "The Decline of the Party in Single-Party African States," in Joseph LaPalombara and Myron Weiner, eds., *Political Parties and Political Development*, Princeton: Princeton University Press, 1966, 201–214.
10. Ibid. See also Henry Bienen, "Political Parties and Political Machines in Africa," in Michael Lofchie, ed., *The State of the Nations*, Berkeley: University of California Press, 1971, 195–213. James Coleman and Carl Rosberg, "African One-party States and Modernization," in Claude Welch Jr., 2nd. ed., *Political Modernization*, Belmont, Mass.: Duxbury Press, 1971, 330–354.
11. Jacques Mariel Nzouankeu, *Les Partis Politiques Sénégalais*, Dakar: Editions Claireafrique, 1984, 13–14 (my translation).
12. Goran Therborn, "The Rule of Capital and the Rise of Democracy," in David Held et al., eds., *States and Societies*, New York: New York University Press, 1983, 261–271.
13. Charles E. Lindblom, *Politics and Markets*, New York: Basic Books, 1977. Seymour Martin Lipset, *Political Man*, Baltimore: The Johns Hopkins University Press, 1981. Walter Rostow, *The Stages of Economic Growth*, Cambridge: Cambridge University Press, 1960. Joseph Schumpeter, *Capitalism, Socialism and Democracy*, 3rd. ed., New York: Harper Brothers, 1975.
14. Lipset, *Political Man*, 31. From a similar perspective, Lindblom argues in *Politics and Markets*: "However poorly the market is

harnessed to democratic purposes only within market-oriented systems does political democracy arise. Not all market-oriented systems are democratic, but every democratic system is also a market-oriented system. Apparently, for reasons not wholly understood, political democracy has been unable to exist except when coupled with the market. An extraordinary proposition, it has so far held without exception." (p. 116).

15. Therborn, "The Rule of Capital and the Rise of Democracy," 270.

16. Ibid., 271.

17. Ibid. See also: Fernando Henrique Cardoso and Enzo Faletto, *Dependency and Development in Latin America*, Berkeley: University of California Press, 1979. David Collier, "Overview of the Bureaucratic-Authoritarian Model," in David Collier, ed., *The New Authoritarianism in Latin America*, Princeton: Princeton University Press, 1979, 19–32. Guillermo O'Donell, "Tensions in the Bureaucratic-Authoritarian State and the Question of Democracy," in David Collier, ed., *The New Authoritarianism in Latin America*, Princeton: Princeton University Press, 1979, 285–318.

18. Samuel P. Huntington, *Political Order in Changing Societies*, New Haven: Yale University Press, 1968; and "Political Development and Political Decay," in Claude Welch Jr., 2nd. ed., *Political Modernization*, Belmont, Mass.: Duxbury Press, 1971, 238–277.

19. Ibid.

20. Michael Lofchie, "Representative Government, Bureaucracy, and Political Development: The African Case," in Marion E. Doro and Newell M. Stultz, eds., *Governing in Black Africa*, Englewood, New Jersey: Prentice Hall, 1970, 282, 289, 294.

21. Robert Jackson and Carl Rosberg, *Personal Rule in Black Africa*, Berkeley: University of California Press, 1982.

22. Juan Linz, *Crisis, Breakdown and Reequilibration*, Baltimore: The Johns Hopkins University Press, 1978.

23. Jackson and Rosberg, *Personal Rule in Black Africa*, 3.

24. Ibid., 73–82.

25. Ibid., 12.

26. Ibid., 77–78, 89–96.

27. Edward J. Schumacher, *Politics, Bureaucracy, and Rural Development in Senegal*, Berkeley: University of California Press, 1975, 5.

28. Jackson and Rosberg, *Personal Rule in Black Africa*, 78.

29. Ibid., 84.

30. Max Weber, *Economy and Society,* edited by Guenther Roth and Claus Wittich, Berkeley: University of California Press, 1978, 246.

31. Karl Marx, *The Marx-Engels Reader*, edited by Robert C. Tucker, New York: W.W. Norton & Company, 1972, 437.

32. Goran Hyden, *No Shorcuts to Progress,* Berkeley: University of California Press, 1983, 8–29.

33. Albert Hirschman, *Essays in Trespassing: Economics to Politics and Beyond*, Cambridge: Cambridge University Press, 1981, 211–265.

34. Hyden, *No Shorcuts to Progress*, 8.

35. Ibid., 7–8.

36. Ibid., 36–45.

37. Ibid., 44.

38. Gunnar Myrdal, *The Challenge of World Poverty*, New York: Vintage Books, 1970, 208–220.

39. Ake, *A Political Economy of Africa*, 181.

40. Paul Harrison, *Inside the Third World*, 2nd ed., New York: Penguin Books, 1981, 383.

41. R. H. Green, "Magendo in the Political Economy of Uganda," *Discussion Paper 164, Institute for Development Studies*, University of Sussex, August 1981. Nelson Kasfir, "State, Magendo, and Class Formation in Uganda," in Nelson Kasfir, ed., *State and Class in Africa*, London: Frank Cass, 1984, 84–103. Richard Sandbrook, *The Politics of Africa's Economic Stagnation*, New York: Cambridge University Press, 1985, 139–144.

42. Kasfir, "State, Magendo, and Class Formation in Uganda," 95.

43. P. Geschiere, "La Paysannerie Africaine est-elle Captive? Sur la Thèse de Goran Hyden, et Pour une Réponse plus Nuancée," *Politique Africaine*, No. 14, (1984), 13–33.

44. Robert H. Bates, *Markets and States in Tropical Africa. The Political Basis of Agricultural Policies*, Berkeley: University of California Press, 1981, 87.

45. Antonio Gramsci, *Selections From the Prison Notebooks*, edited and translated by Quintin Hoare and Geoffrey Nowell Smith, London: Lawrence and Wishart, 1971, 52.

46. Ibid., 12.

47. Hirscham, *Essays in Trespassing*.

48. Ibid., 224.

49. Gramsci, *Selections from the Prison Notebooks*.

50. Weber, *Economy and Society*, 212, 263.

51. Thomas M. Callaghy, *The State-Society Struggle. Zaire in Comparative Perspective*, New York: Columbia University Press, 1984, 173–184, 318–330. Crawford Young, *Ideology and Development in Africa*, New Haven: Yale University Press, 1982.

52. Ake, *A Political Economy of Africa*. Samir Amin, *Accumulation on a World Scale*, New York: Monthly Review Press, 1974. Cardoso and Faletto, *Dependency and Development in Latin America* . Peter Evans, *Dependent Development*, Princeton: Princeton University Press, 1979. André Gunder Frank, *Crisis: In the Third World*, New York: Holmes and Meier Publishers, 1981.

53. Ibid. See also Walter Rodney, *How Europe Underdeveloped Africa*, Washington: Howard University Press, 1972. Immanuel Wallerstein, *The Capitalist World Economy*, Cambridge: Cambridge

University Press, 1979.

54. Clive Thomas, *Dependence and Transformation*, New York: Monthly Review Press, 1974.

55. Arghiri Emmanuel, *Unequal Exchange*, New York: Monthly Review Press, 1972.

56. Frank, *Crisis: In the Third World*, 230–279.

57. Martin Carnoy, *The State and Political Theory*, Princeton: Princeton University Press, 1984, 172–207.

58. Frank, *Crisis: In the Third World*, 231.

59. Monique Anson-Meyer, *Mécanismes de l'Exploitation en Afrique. L'Exemple du Sénégal*, La Rochelle: Editions Cujas, 1974. Amin, *Accumulation on a World Scale*. Frank, *Crisis: In the Third World*.

60. Frank, *Crisis: In the Third World*, 230–231.

61. Ibid., 230.

62. Clive Thomas, *The Rise of the Authoritarian State in Peripheral Societies*, New York: Monthly Review Press, 1984, 88.

63. Fernando Henrique Cardoso, "On the Characterization of Authoritarian Regimes in Latin America," in David Collier, ed., *The New Authoritarianism in Latin America*, Princeton: Princeton University Press, 1979. Collier, "Overview of the Bureaucratic-Authoritarian Model." O'Donnell, "Tensions in the Bureaucratic-Authoritarian State and the Question of Democracy." Sandbrook, *The Politics of Africa's Economic Stagnation*. Nicola Swainson, *The Development of Corporate Capitalism in Kenya, 1918–1977*, Berkeley: University of California Press, 1980.

64. Cardoso and Faletto, *Dependency and Development in Latin America*, XVI.

65. O'Donnell, "Tensions in the Bureaucratic-Authoritarian Model and the Question of Democracy," 292.

66. Alfred Stepan, *The State and Society*, Princeton: Princeton University Press, 1978.

67. O'Donnell, "Tensions in the Bureaucratic-Authoritarian Model and the Question of Democracy."

68. Collier, "Overview of the Bureaucratic-Authoritarian Model."

69. Claude Ake, *Revolutionary Pressures in Africa*, London: Zed Press, 1978, 78.

70. Samir Amin, *Le Monde des Affaires Sénégalais*, Paris: Editions de Minuit; *Neo-colonialism in West Africa*, Harmondsworth: Penguin Books, 1973. Anson-Meyer, *Mécanismes de l'Exploitation en Afrique. L'Exemple du Sénégal*. Sheldon Gellar, *Senegal: An African Nation Between Islam and the West*, Boulder: Westview Press, 45–66.

71. Rita Cruise O'Brien, *The Political Economy of Underdevelopment: Dependence in Senegal*, Beverly Hills: Sage Publications, 1979.

72. Samir Amin, "The Development of the Senegalese Business Bourgeoisie," in Adebayo Adedeji, ed., *Indigenization of African Economies*, London: Hutchinson University Library, 1981, 320. Rita

Cruise O'Brien, "Foreign Ascendance in the Economy and State: The French and Lebanese," in Rita Cruise O'Brien, ed., *The Political Economy of Underdevelopment: Dependence in Senegal,* Beverly Hills: Sage Publications, 1979.

3

Organic Crisis, Organic Intellectuals, and the Senegalese Passive Revolution

Senegal's process of liberalization, initiated under the strong presidential rule of Léopold Sédar Senghor in 1974 and completed by his successor Abdou Diouf in 1981, transformed the de facto one-party state of the Union progressiste sénégalaise (UPS) into a liberal democracy. In less than ten years, the authoritarian structures of Senegal's political system were gradually changed to accommodate the introduction of a rigid tripartite system of governance that soon generated the legalization of all political parties irrespective of their ideological orientation.[1] This process of liberalization should be interpreted as a ruling class project intended to reorganize the state by diffusing an "organic crisis" and neutralizing the threat from the Left.

In response to the crisis, liberalization consisted in "preventing the development of a revolutionary adversary by 'decapitating' its revolutionary potential."[2] Accordingly, the Senegalese ruling class project represents what Antonio Gramsci called a passive revolution. The Senegalese ruling class expressed its hegemony by having exchanged force and authoritarianism as its method of governance for the politics of alliances and cooptation. Indeed, it asserted its hegemony because it defended its interests by universalizing them, and ensuring that they could "become the interests of the ... subordinate groups."[3] Although authoritarianism was displaced by the politics of hegemony, the structures of power remained fundamentally unchanged. This is precisely why the democratization of Senegal should be viewed as a successful passive revolution.

Gramsci's notion of passive revolution derives from the conservative Italian intellectual, Vincenzo Cuoco, who asserted that society had to change if it were to preserve its most fundamental structures.[4] Accordingly, a passive revolution is a preemptive response from "on high" to the disorganized but potentially revolutionary demands of dominated classes. It is the specific peaceful means of survival of a ruling class in conditions of organic crisis. According to Gramsci, "These incessant and persistent efforts [to stem a political crisis] ... form the terrain of the 'conjunctural,' and it is upon this terrain that the forces of opposition organise."[5]

The terrain of the conjunctural, however, has "no far-reaching historical significance," despite its being the arena of immediate political and economic struggles.[6] Of much greater significance is the organic crisis that relates to a crisis of total structures and engenders what Stuart Hall has called the "formative efforts" of the ruling class.[7] These formative efforts, to paraphrase Hall, are an attempt to forge a new balance of forces and propel the emergence of new elements. They seek to put together a new historical bloc, as well as new political configurations and philosophies. Formative efforts involve, therefore, a profound restructuring of the state and the ideological discourse that construct the crisis and represent it as a practical reality. Consequently, new programs and policies pointing to a new result, a new sort of settlement—within certain limits—are required. "These do not 'emerge': they have to be constructed. Political and ideological work is required to disarticulate old formations, and to rework their elements into new configurations."[8] The democratization of Senegal embodied therefore the formative efforts of a ruling class confronting the organic crisis generated by the contradictions of peripheral capitalism.

In this sense, the process of democratization that congealed as a passive revolution constituted the search for and the construction of a hegemonic project. Ernesto Laclau and Chantal Mouffe observe:

> 'Hegemony' will allude to an absent totality, and to the diverse attempts at recomposition and rearticulation which, in overcoming this original absence, made it possible for struggles to be given a meaning and for historical forces to be endowed with full positivity. The contexts in which the concept appear will be those of a fault ... of a fissure that had to be filled up, of a contingency that had to be overcome. 'Hegemony' will

be not the majestic unfolding of an identity but the response to a crisis.[9]

This chapter is an analysis of the Senegalese crisis and of how "organic intellectuals" filled a fundamental hiatus in ruling class power by constructing the ideological, political, socioeconomic, and cultural configurations of a new hegemony. It seeks to demonstrate both the crucial importance of such intellectuals in elaborating and legitimating the formative efforts of the ruling class and the structural limitations to the implementation of these constructs.

The Organic Crisis

The concept of organic crisis reflects Gramsci's idea that, at certain moments in history, society confronts a crisis that engulfs the totality of its structures. Authority is delegitimated, old values disintegrate, the economy is paralyzed, the rule of the ruling class is almost exclusively sustained by force, the dominated classes no longer put up with their subaltern status, and the state can hardly preserve the social continuity of life. Such general decay of the existing order occurs

> either because the ruling class has failed in some major political undertaking for which it has requested, or forcibly extracted, the consent of the broad masses ... or because huge masses ... have passed suddenly from a state of political passivity to a certain activity, and put forward demands which taken together, albeit not organically formulated, add up to a revolution. A 'crisis of authority' is spoken of: this is precisely the crisis of hegemony, or general crisis of the State.[10]

In Senegal, the general crisis of the state was characterized by the incapacity of Senghor's regime to resolve the acute economic, political, and social contradictions generated by a dependent form of capitalist underdevelopment. The promises of independence had failed to materialize; material growth and prosperity had not crystallized; foreign forces still controlled the fundamental sectors of production, as well as the vital positions of the bureaucracy; and the ideology of socialist *négritude* could not mask the ugly realities of persistent inequalities and growing corruption. Thus, in spite of independence, the overall structures of Senegalese society remained denationalized.

The first decade of Senghor's rule was marked by a continuity of past colonial economic policies.[11] The Senegalese state merely nationalized the public institutions of the colonial era and a few newly created agencies of development.[12] The industrial sector remained firmly under the domination of French capital. Agriculture constituted the main sector for state intervention as Senghor's regime pursued a policy bent on giving priority to the production of peanuts. In the name of socialism, the private marketing of peanuts was gradually abolished: the state imposed its direct control over the rural economy by creating the Office de commercialisation agricole (OCA) in the early days of independence, and then the Office national de coopération et d'assistance au développement (ONCAD) in 1966.

The priority given to agriculture and the peanut in particular is not surprising. As N. Casswell elaborates:

> At the time of independence, peanut production represented, alone, more than 80 percent of the country's exports. Peanut cultivation employed 87 percent of the active population and covered half of the cultivated land.... Senegal's dependence on the peanut, however, was not merely confined to the rural sector. The processing of peanut represented 42 percent of the turnover of Senegalese industry as a whole, and a substantial part of the budgetary revenues of the former colony derived from taxes on the exportation of this product. The powerful Muslim leaders also owed a good part of their wealth and power to the peanut sector, just as the ruling party had very consciously courted the peasant electorate of the peanut basin.... Let us add to this the fact that the quasi-totality of the harvest was exported to France where it supplied 60 percent of the total consumption of vegetable oil, and we will understand better the strategic importance of this product, not only for the Senegalese economy, but also for the political control of the country.[13]

The creation of OCA and ONCAD rested initially on the belief that state control of the rural sector would result in the liberation of the peasantry from its chronic burdens of debts to French commercial houses and rich Lebanese middlemen.[14] In addition, OCA and ONCAD were supposed to become the vehicle by which peasants would acquire the resources and skills that would allow them to set up autonomous, self-sufficient, and modern cooperatives. OCA and ONCAD, in other words, were to establish the structures of their own dissolution.[15] Such a vision of peasant socialism disappeared rapidly in the aftermath of Prime Minister Dia's ouster, and Senghor's increasingly conservative consolidation of power.[16]

OCA was dissolved in 1967; its functions were ultimately transferred to ONCAD, which became a massive bureaucratic organ of resource extraction from the countryside to the privileged urban sector. Such extractions contributed to the growing disparities of wealth between the peasant periphery and the bureaucratic center. The bureaucrats, representing about 3 percent of the total active population, received 46 percent of state expenditures, and their average salary was seven times higher than that of a peasant and two times higher than that of a skilled worker.[17]

Through its manipulation of trade policies and its control over marketing and transport, ONCAD—until 1974–1975, when the tendency was reversed—subsidized the cost of food and thus appeased the interests of foreign capital seeking a lower wage bill, as well as those of urban workers bent on preserving their standard of living.[18] Casswell says further that

> the peanut sector supplied a substantial amount of the State's budgetary receipts.... The benefits of ONCAD through the Fund for Price Stabilization were systematically used to subsidize the price of rice and, thus, urban salaries....[19]

The problem of peasant exploitation was seriously exacerbated when, in 1967, France abolished its price supports to Senegalese peanut exports.[20] The government, burdened by increasing state expenditures for a voracious and growing bureaucracy, responded by lowering the official producer's price for peanut by 15 percent.[21] In addition, the rural sector was plagued by bad weather conditions, which crippled the harvests of 1966 and 1968.[22] Finally, far from alleviating the peasants' debts, ONCAD contributed not only to their increase but also to their stricter collection.[23]

ONCAD, however, played a significant political role by consolidating the rural power of the Islamic leaders, the *marabouts*. The *marabouts* were granted special privileges and rights that contributed to the expansion of their material, as well as spiritual control over their peasant disciples, the *taalibes*. They enjoyed a preferential status that authorized them to sell their private harvests at higher prices and that granted them a larger allocation of fertilizers and seeds. They also benefited from special lines of credits, as well as from the "tolerance" of the state in terms of the repayments of their debts.[24] With the help of the state, the *marabouts* were becoming rural entrepreneurs with vested interests in the preservation of the status quo. This is not to say that their spiritual role had been replaced by their emerging status as a rural bourgeoisie. On the contrary, this new status reinforced their spiritual aura, as well as their patronage capacity. Moreover, because the state depended on them to maintain the stability of the countryside, they possessed a certain autonomy from the public authorities which allowed them to defend (within certain limits) the interests of their peasant disciples. As Christian Coulon details:

> Seen from above, from the 'summit' of the state, [the *marabouts*] are slightly embarassing allies, notables who are too autonomous and whom the state would like to do without, but whom it cannot easily brush aside without political risks. Seen from below, in the everyday life of the *taalibes*, they are, more than ever, popular heroes, indispensable protectors, and the guardians of the 'citadel of good.'[25]

The popular perception of the *marabouts* as guardians of the collective good was strongly reinforced by their defense of peasant interests when deteriorating rural conditions precipitated what was officially designated as the *malaise paysan*. The *malaise paysan* symbolized the rural sector's resistance to governmental policies and its retrenchment into subsistence production.

> The peasants responded ... by withdrawing from rural development services, intensifying noncompliance with administrative regulations and laws, and shifting from peanut cultivation to subsistence farming. Beginning with the severe drought of 1968, governmental officials reported sharp increases in the production of millet for local consumption in acreage previously devoted to peanuts.... In addition, the clandestine flow of peanuts across the Gambian and Guinean borders was generally estimated by 1970 to have risen to an annual level of forty thousand to fifty thousand tons; and within Senegal there was mounting evidence of widespread tax evasion and illicit speculation in peanuts....
> Perhaps the most disturbing form of rural protest from the

viewpoint of governmental leaders was the tendency of farmers throughout the central peanut-producing zone to refuse to repay seed peanut and agricultural equipment loans.[26]

In spite of being alleviated in the mid-1970s by the introduction of greater incentives to farmers, the *malaise paysan* was to remain a persistent feature of the Senegalese political economy.[27] It culminated in 1980 with the abolition of ONCAD and the government's acknowledgment that its agricultural policies had failed. While ONCAD provided the means to lower the urban incomes and thus maintain the profitability of industry, it did not liberate the peasantry from exploitation and indebtedness. In fact, the state replaced the old colonial houses and Lebanese middlemen as the central source of peasant subjection and affliction. The peasantry, however, remained relatively "uncaptured" and escaped from the total control of the state; it established parallel markets and networks of commercialization.[28] Therefore, it had certain means to resist state exploitation and policies. As Casswell noted:

The disastrous harvest of 1980–1981, the worst since World War II, marked the virtual collapse of the official network of commercialization: less than half of the estimated production passed through the network, and the repayment of debts represented only 2.2 percent of the amount due. On 31 October 1980, ONCAD ceased to exist, leaving a debt of 90 billion francs CFA. Three months later, the government, in an effort to reestablish peasant confidence, raised the official price of peanuts from fifty to seventy francs a kilo, and canceled or suspended a rural debt totalling 31.9 billion francs CFA.[29]

ONCAD's role had thus changed: from being a source of subsidies to the urban sectors it became a burden on them.[30] Its failure in continuing to transfer resources from the countryside to industry and the state bureaucracy explains in part its final demise; it is clear that ONCAD was greatly responsible for the persisting *malaise paysan* that contributed to the exacerbation of the organic crisis of Senegalese peripheral capitalism.

Peasant discontent, however, was not the only cause of the organic crisis. The aspiring Senegalese bourgeoisie, the powerless technocratic elite, the frustrated intellectuals and students, and the repressed working class were all profoundly dissatisfied with the fruits of the first decade of independence. This dissatisfaction crystallized in May and June of 1968 in a wave of strikes and violent confrontations that profoundly shook Senghor's regime.[31]

The events of 1968 resulted from the pervasive feeling among all social classes that independence had failed to bring them the benefits that it entailed. The government had been incapable of generating structures of empowerment for the aspiring bourgeoisie: French capital still controlled the dominant sectors of industry, and commerce was in the hands of the Lebanese. It is in these circumstances that this bourgeoisie created, in 1968, a small pressure group, l'Union des groupements économiques du Sénégal (UNIGES), to confront the government with several demands:

> In an almost threatening tone, [the UNIGES] called for an africanization of the consultative assemblies, a large expansion of credit facilities, a preference in administrative commands, and even the institution of virtual monopolies in diverse branches of activities for the benefit of Senegalese nationals.[32]

The Senegalese bourgeoisie was calling for the necessary conditions conducive to its crystallization as a national and independent bourgeoisie. Such demands, however, did not represent a frontal assault on Senghor himself and his regime. In fact, members of the UNIGES organized public meetings celebrating Senghor's sixty-second birthday and pledged fidelity to the institutions that he had come to incarnate.[33] What the aspiring bourgeoisie demanded was just a better deal and the state-induced opportunities for its economic advancement. These opportunities, however, were difficult to materialize since the policies of import-substitution, pursued during the first decade of independence, implied an inevitable reliance on foreign and, in particular, French capital. In these circumstances, the state was more interested in attracting multinational firms than in creating a strong Senegalese private sector—after a decade of independence, this sector had not developed beyond the artisanal stage.[34] In addition, the economy had little space for a Senegalese bourgeoisie since it was dominated by alien forces: in 1970, Europeans controlled or owned 47 of the 49 key financial institutions of the country, as well as 56 percent of the 1,600 most important commercial firms. Those firms under Senegalese control were most often connected to French and/or other expatriate capital.[35]

After a decade of independence, the Senghorian regime had failed to "Senegalize" the economy and develop independent and integrated structures of growth. Guy Rocheteau describes this phenomenon:

> The national objective of industrialization through import-substitution has given rise to new industrial activities ... but in most cases they have been initiated by traditional French suppliers to Africa, who substituted the exportation of capital for the exportation of goods. The more intense prospecting and exploitation of Senegalese natural resources ... has not excluded an effort at local industrial 'valorization' before exportation ... but the markets remain principally french and continue to depend on agreements regulating the share of external markets between industries located in France and overseas. The beginning of an internationalization of production in the exploitation of lime phosphates and of oil prospecting has not fundamentally changed this pattern, insofar as it only represents the transposition to the domestic level of the competition between large European firms for control of the world markets.[36]

The economy was not the only area suffering from foreign dominance; the educational system and, in particular, the university, as well as the top echelons of the bureaucracy, had remained under the strong control of French advisers. Not surprisingly, Senegalese students and teachers, frustrated by a French *blocage*, and inevitably influenced by the revolutionary winds of change that had blown from campuses from Paris to Berkeley, revolted at the end of May 1968. Both university and secondary school students went on strike to oppose the continuing hegemony of French culture and capital, and to condemn the government for its neocolonial character.[37] On 27 May, the government called on the army to suppress student unrest; on 29 May, the university was placed under military control, while the lycées of Dakar, Saint-Louis and Thiès were closed.

Such repressive actions, however, united students and workers whose trade union, the UNTS (Union nationale des travailleurs sénégalais), called for a general and unlimited strike on 31 May. The strike, in spite of its success in Dakar and the Cap-Vert region, was very rapidly put down by the coercive apparatus of the state, which had remained loyal to Senghor.[38] In addition, Senghor could again depend for his survival on both the French Fifth Republic, which had reestablished its hegemony after the turbulent events of May 1968, and the *marabouts* who had clearly committed themselves to his defense by firmly condemning the opposition as composed of *contestataires* and *fauteurs de trouble*.[39] Supported by the army and the spiritual leaders of the peasantry, and having received the discreet military protection of the French, Senghor regained the upper hand and embarked on a mixed strategy of concession and repression.[40] The strategy was bent on dividing the opposition and, in particular, the emerging alliance between workers and students.

Senghor demarcated clearly the workers' demands from those of the students. While he dismissed the latter as illegitimate and originating from subversive foreign forces, he saw in the former genuine grievances that had to be redressed.[41] On 12 June, a tripartite conference between the government, labor, and capital resulted in certain significant gains for workers: the minimum wage, which had been frozen since 1961, was increased by more than 15 percent, a system of price controls was established to sustain living standards, and health services were to be partially paid by employers.[42] Although these concessions alleviated the plight of the working class, they did not immediately eliminate discontent. Labor relations became less volatile and confrontational only when a progovernment faction dissolved the UNTS in August 1969, and created the CNTS (Confédération nationale des travailleurs du Sénégal) as a docile affiliate of the UPS. The integration of the CNTS into the political structures of Senghor's regime inaugurated the period of *la participation responsable*.[43]

The Senghorian state survived the organic crisis of the late 1960s, which had been caused by the combined discontent of the countryside and the urban areas. This was not only due to its control over the coercive apparatus and its alliance with maraboutic power, it was also a reflection of the contradictory, disorganized, and leaderless character of the forces of the opposition. The defeat of these forces was probably the result of their incapacity to bridge their differences and elaborate a coherent and united revolutionary strategy. According to Pierre Fougeyrollas,

> the divergences in the opposition were quite evident: the students
> hoped for the institution of a Castro-like revolutionary regime,
> the wage earners and civil servants most hostile to

President Senghor longed for a change of head of state and accepted the prospects—dismissed by the students—of a transitional military government. As for the peasants, their discontent with and disregard for the public authorities did not prevent them from dreading adventure even more than the maintenance of the existing order.[44]

The crisis, however, created dangers and opportunities for both rulers and ruled, and it heralded a period of great uncertainties and conflicts.[45] Gramsci explains that

if the ruling class has lost its consensus, i.e., is no longer 'leading' but only 'dominant,' exercising coercive force alone, this means precisely that the great masses have become detached from their traditional ideologies, and no longer believe what they used to believe previously.... The crisis consists precisely in the fact that the old is dying and the new cannot be born; in this interregnum a great variety of morbid symptoms appear.[46]

The organic crisis was thus a reflection of the ruling class's incapacity to "lead" and a function of the mounting challenges and disenchantment of the subaltern classes. But it remained just a crisis precisely because these subaltern classes were divided, disorganized, and in disarray. In these circumstances, it is not surprising that the ruling class, which still controlled the coercive apparatus of the state and the most important organs of cultural and ideological dissemination, was in a better situation than its popular challengers to reassert and recreate its hegemony. Such reassertion, however, required the ruling class to make certain sacrifices and elaborate a formative strategy. The substance of this formative strategy is the topic of the next section.

Formative Strategy and Organic Intellectuals

The formative efforts of the ruling class were rooted in the need to create a new hegemony capable of legitimating the Senghorian state. In other words, the ruling class had to reestablish its leadership at the ideological and cultural levels to neutralize popular challenges and, indeed, gain the consent of the broad masses. Therefore, it had to develop its own "organic intellectuals" to direct and organize its world-view and aspirations.

> Every social group, coming into existence on the original terrain
> of an essential function in the world of economic production,
> creates together with itself, organically, one or more strata of
> intellectuals which give it homogeneity and an awareness of its
> own function not only in the economic but also in the social and
> political fields.
> .... The intellectuals are the dominant group's 'deputies'
> exercising the subaltern functions of social hegemony and
> political government.[47]

In this perspective, organic intellectuals are managers of
legitimation, they contribute to making the class to which they
belong into the leading and hegemonic class of society. They
disseminate the dominant ideology to integrate the subordinate
classes into the bourgeois way of life. They represent the
political practices embodying the hierarchical relationship
between subaltern and ruling classes as constitutive of the
"general interest."

> This is the most purely political phase, and marks the decisive
> passage from the structure to the sphere of the complex
> superstructure; it is the phase in which previously germinated
> ideologies become 'party,' come into confrontation and conflict,
> until only one of them, or at least a single combination of them,
> tends to prevail, to gain the upper hand, to propagate itself
> throughout society—bringing about not only a unison of
> economic and political aims, but also intellectual and moral unity,
> posing all the questions around which the struggle rages not on a
> corporate but on a 'universal' plane, and thus creating the
> hegemony of a fundamental social group over a series of
> subordinate groups.[48]

Such a process of universalization of corporate class
interests requires the intense labor of cultural imagination,
diffusion, and penetration by the organic intellectuals. It is
such labor that imparts to the masses their proper ideological
code of conduct and beliefs. Senghor had no doubts about this:

> The consciousness of the masses, who lack education and culture,
> still remains confused, lost in the fog of animal needs. It does not
> rise to the level of 'political consciousness, a superior form of
> consciousness.' This can only reach the masses from the outside,
> from the 'intellectuals.'[49]

Intellectuals had, therefore, a significant role to play in the making of the Senegalese passive revolution. As managers of political legitimation and cultural dissemination, they sought to channel and mold popular energies—that is, to control their forms and guide their development.

Regrouped in two centers of mental production, the Club nation et développement du sénégal (CND) and the Centre d'études de recherches et d'éducation socialistes (CERES), founded respectively in March 1969 and August 1970, the organic intellectuals identified the fundamental elements of the organic crisis and proposed a political and economic program for its resolution. The essence of their program rested on the elimination of *la politique politicienne* and its replacement by a technocratic nationalism within a liberalized structure of governance.

Both the CND and the CERES, however, functioned more as loyal and "responsible" critics of the government than as autonomous agents of radical change; they were organically connected to Senghor's regime. The CND was founded in the home of Alioune Sène who was at the time the director of Senghor's cabinet,[50] and it clearly defined its members as *des serviteurs de l'Etat* who knew the limits of the politically permissible.[51] The CERES was even closer to the government since it was the cultural, educational, and ideological organ of the UPS. It played *un rôle positif d'anti-contestation raisonée et un rôle théorique de formation et d'autoformation.*[52]

Thus, criticisms of the institutions of Senghor's regime were to remain loyal and responsible. As defined by one of its members, Joseph Mathiam, the function of the club was to confront the crisis and analyze objectively the circumstances of its origins and persistence; such analysis was to constitute the source of a *"remise en question* and of new initiatives at the theoretical as well as the active level."[53] This *remise en question,* however, did not constitute a challenge to Senghor's regime; in fact, it demanded the social and political realization of "Senghorism" itself. As Mathiam put it:

> In the current conjuncture of Senegalese politics, one man plays a major strategic role because of the institutions, as well as because of his influence and place in history. This man appears to be isolated and lonely, or poorly advised, which is even worse. Burdened with problems of planning and execution, this man, open to dialogue and cooperation, leads his compatriots

into a permanent debate over Senegal's present and future.

This is why the club intends to institute with the head of state an unequivocal collaboration within the context of this great debate, and thus contribute to the unity of all the active forces of Senegal.[54]

In this perspective, Senghor was above criticism; the failures of his regime were those of his entourage and of modern imperialism, they were neither of his making, nor of his socialist *négritude*.[55] Yet, the failures were generalized and they indeed constituted an organic crisis; they were rooted in weak and unbalanced material structures and they affected society as a whole.[56] Doudou Gueye, a member of the club, identified three fundamental and profound deficiencies in the Senegalese political economy:

1. Deficiencies in the exercise of our sovereignty, which lead progressively to a situation ... of acute impotence.
2. Economic stagnation [resulting from:]
   a. Foreign control of the Senegalese economy;
   b. The abortion of Senegalese private and even public initiatives.
   c. This situation is inevitable; it is caused by the obdurate limitations set by the structures and institutions of foreign capital.
3. Deficiencies in authentic democratic practices; in this instance, it is necessary to insist and to declare that authentic democratic practices have yet to be realized[:]
   a. The people of our nation in whom rest all the potentialities of our global development cannot participate spontaneously, in an effective and active manner, in the fundamental processes of decision making because they are absent from the cultural and intellectual forms of representation, and thus cannot take part in the actual elaboration of ideas.
   b. The de facto elites ... have been content to 'satellize' themselves on a modernist orbit totally foreign to the people ...; in this orbit, the elites are alienated and incapable of integrating themselves into any system of popular representation....[57]

Senegal's problem was its dependence on uncontrollable external forces, which perverted its cultural autonomy, denationalized its elite, and corrupted its democracy. Not surprisingly, the club's solution to the crisis rested on the adoption of a series of policies destined to simultaneously strengthen and improve the administrative structures of the state and democratize political life. These policies, however, depended on the succesful elaboration of a "myth" capable of motivating both the intellectual cadres and the masses. In the given historical conjuncture of Senegal this myth had to be rooted in a *prise de conscience nationale,* inspired and conditioned by a modernized version of socialist *négritude.*[58] Such *prise de conscience* was neither spontaneous nor inevitable; it required the intense labor of the intellectual cadres. Without them, the masses would never acquire the will and motivation necessary for their own liberation.

In these circumstances, the club saw itself as a vehicle of social criticism, cultural dissemination, and political formation. Its intellectuals were to reactualize *la négritude* or, to put it more bluntly, to legitimize "Senghorism" as a coherent and popular ideology of development. Babacar Ba said, "The cadres are the natural vectors of ideology. It is up to them to enlighten and guide the popular masses, to bring them this minimum of awareness and lucidity without which any action is inconceivable."[59]

In this sense, the organic intellectuals of Senegal's passive revolution articulated a profoundly elitist ideology of development. While their vision was broadly nationalistic, it was also hierarchical and paternalistic; indeed, although it sought to introduce substantial changes in the political economy, it failed to challenge the traditional division between rulers and ruled. The popular sectors were to remain "passive" insofar as their incorporation into the new structures of the state was to be directed and guided from "above." As envisaged by the organic intellectuals, the reorganization of Senegalese society was an ideological and technical process, and consequently, it was their own affair. Doudou Gueye explains such sentiments as follows:

> In our historical conditions, national consciousness ... postulates an active attitude. It cannot correspond to a spontaneous attitude.... And it is because it is active that it can constitute the key to stop the infernal cycle to which our underdevelopment and the will of the developed and wealthy countries seem to condemn us.
>
> This active attitude cannot be an act of the people ... because the people lack the cultural and intellectual capacity to plan and initiate programs leading to modernization.[60]

For the organic intellectuals, only they and the modern cadres of the state bureaucracy could play a leadership role; they saw themselves as the bearers of the new hegemony. This is not to say that they ignored the aspirations of the subaltern classes, but rather that these aspirations were to be rendered harmless by cooptation into the institutions of the ruling groups. Indeed, the agenda, demands, and ideology of the masses would not be threatening to the foundations of the existing social relations of power since all of them would be formulated by the organic intellectuals. This Senghor understood well, for as he succinctly put it, "It is up to the intellectuals to apprehend the revolution to lead to it."[61]   Thus, the political autonomy and independence of the popular sectors would be severely restrained by the hegemony of the ruling class and its organic intellectuals.

This lack of political autonomy would also reflect the ruling class's new capacity of absorption, assimilation, and direction of subaltern groups. It would demonstrate that the organic crisis could be resolved within the perimeters of the basic structures of the Senghorian state. Gramsci pointed out long ago that

> a social form 'always' has marginal possibilities for further development and organisational improvement, and in particular can count on the relative weakness of the rival progressive force as a result of its specific character and way of life. It is necessary for the dominant social form to preserve this weakness....[62]

Looked at this way, the organic intellectuals of the Senegalese passive revolution were cognizant of the deficiencies of the subaltern classes and of the leadership capacities of a reformed ruling class. This is why Doudou Gueye claimed that the mental labor of the club had to "lead to the weakening of the existing elites. Their efforts to reimpose their authority will transform them into true elites capable of assuming their responsibilities ... and because they will have become true elites, they will make these fundamental responsibilities identifiable to the masses and by the masses.[63]

Obviously, the organic intellectuals believed in the hegemonic capacity of the Senegalese ruling class and indeed in its potential for organizing and elaborating an ideology acceptable at all levels of society. Put another way, the ruling class's interests, world views, and aspirations could be made congruent with those of the subaltern masses. Its hegemony could become real, it would not just be the product of a hard process of intellectual dissemination and diffusion. Colonialism, the organic intellectuals suggested, created the historical conditions for non-antagonistic and true complementary relations between the different strata of the Senegalese nation. The notion of the nation as a non-contradictory social whole stemmed from the realities of colonial and neocolonial dependence. As Babacar Ba explains, in Senegal the historical reality of external dominance disturbed the normal process of class formation and class antagonism:

> The external factor was colonization: our 'working class' was its product; it was created by foreign capital. Its existence and that of the young national bourgeoisie are not dialectically linked. Thus, their interests, far from being contradictory, are fully convergent.
>
> It is important to quickly clarify that this young national bourgeoisie, taking into account its weakness and its limited influence in our economic life, does not yet truly 'exist'; it aspires to be, and it has the potential to be.
>
> It is as if there existed next to the peasantry and the 'working class' a Senegalese bourgeoisie of European stock and a Lebanese-Syrian middle class. Yes, our young national bourgeoisie, as a class of producers or businessmen, has never really been 'involved.' Quite the contrary, it has always been carefully kept 'on the sidelines.' Its aspirations and its demands coincide essentially with those of the majority of the nation. In this sense, it is a bearer of progress; it finds itself in its ascending phase; it is not only national but also nationalistic.[64]

In these circumstances, it is not surprising to discover that for the organic intellectuals the process of democratization that they advocated represented a means of transforming the governing elite into a true ruling class. In other words, it would be the process through which this elite would gain its ascendancy as the directing head of all the national forces. This implied that the elite would identify its own interests and aspirations, as well as those of the subaltern groups, to bring about "not only a unison of economic and political aims, but also intellectual and moral unity, posing all the questions around which the struggle rages not on a corporate but on a 'universal' plane."[65]

The Senegalese ruling class would create its own hegemony, and such a task would be facilitated by the alleged classlessness of Senegalese society. The process of nation building would be non-antagonistic, for as Doudou Ngom, the president of the Confédération nationale des travailleurs du sénégal, reminded the working class, for the "concept of class interest we have substituted that of national interest."[66] In addition, the national interest required that the aspiring Senegalese bourgeoisie be given a special role in the governing party. President Senghor explained why this was so:

> Why is the UPS, a socialist party, interested in bourgeois classes, and why does it intend to give them a specific representation or, to put it more precisely, a supplementary representation in the party? The answer is simple: because the UPS is, at the same time, a national party, because nation building is the sine qua non condition of all development, whether socialist or not.[67]

The process of nation building, in turn, required the creation of an "integral state" capable of controlling directly the economic, ideological, and political direction of Senegalese society without the help of transmissive organs of power such as the *marabouts*. As Jean Copans remarked in 1980:

> Today we are entering a new phase, where the domination of the ruling classes demands that all means, material and intellectual, be in their hands. We go from a situation where the Murid brotherhood serves as an ideological apparatus of the state, although it does not convey nor practice the ideology of the state and the groups staffing it, to a situation where the state must become the emanation of its own ideological apparatuses. The state does not seek to eliminate or really to further control the brotherhood; it seeks to develop its own instruments of domination.[68]

This new situation of increasing statism embodies the ruling class's effort to construct an integral state. The integral state represents the rise of the technostructure whose goal is the multiplication of state interventions in domains that had hitherto been neglected and/or considered politically out of reach. The emphasis is on the technocratic management of the developmental process at the expense of the traditional clientelism of *la politique politicienne*.[69] This transition to a new structure of governance was initiated in 1970 with the appointment of Abdou Diouf, the embodiment of the technostructure, to the recreated office of prime minister and with the deconcentration of presidential power. As the immediate goal of these reforms was the protection of Senghor from direct popular criticism, Diouf would now have to accept the blame for unpopular and failing policies.[70]

In addition, the deconcentration of Senghor's presidentialism contained the seeds of the process of democratization demanded by the organic intellectuals and the opposition. It signaled the coming to power of the organic intellectuals themselves, as several founding members of the CND integrated the governing structures of the UPS and the state.[71] The Senegalese passive revolution had begun.

The Contradictions of the Passive Revolution

The Senghorian Phase

The passive revolution represented a multifaceted project of economic, political, and ideological restructuring of Senegalese society that would crystallize in an integral state. At the economic level, the creation of an integral state implied the intervention of public institutions in the fundamental sectors of industry. The state was to function not only as an agent of growth and as an entrepreneur, it was to provide also the material and structural means conducive to the emergence of a national bourgeoisie.[72] As President Senghor explained in his general political report of December 1969:

> The necessity of constructing transitional phases is a necessity for African socialists lest they launch themselves into romantic adventurism and fail miserably.... It is necessary not only to construct stages, but also to depend on the existing intellectual cadres: on the bourgeois cadres who are currently businessmen and men of liberal professions, government employees of all levels, engineers and technicians, employees and skilled workers—but first of all, on the businessmen and salaried workers....
> It is not a matter of building, today, in 1969–1970, an integral socialist society; it is a matter of moving towards it by stages. Now, we cannot, without doing damage, shortcut the stages and do without first a cultivated, competent, and experienced 'national bourgeoisie.'[73]

Senghor's conception of the transition to bourgeois governance as a necessary stage in the building of socialism stemmed from his acceptance of John Kenneth Galbraith's thesis that power in the modern industrial age was no longer in the hands of the capitalist class or the state, but in those of the technostructure by virtue of its scientific and managerial skills.[74] Such a conception corresponded to an elitist vision of society since wealth, privilege, and status would inevitably be bestowed only on those capable of assimilating and obtaining scientific knowledge. It contributed therefore to the legitimation of inequalities and the persistence of the great divide separating rulers from ruled. In addition, it favored the foreign penetration of the economy, which was perceived as a conveyor of scarce capital and an agent of modernity. Such a penetration did not contradict the process of Senegalization, for economic power rested not on the ownership of the means of production, but on the technostructure's managerial control of industry. As Senghor emphasized:

> We must contribute to the making of a Senegalese class of businessmen and managers—organizers and administrators who will gradually nationalize, as is natural for a nation, the greater part of the national economy....
> The real problem is thus not the expulsion of foreigners. This is neither possible nor desirable. The real problem is to give Senegalese the opportunity to build up enterprises ... producing goods and services at least equal in quantity and quality to those goods and services produced by foreigners. In short, the real problem ... is to offer the Senegalese the technical knowledge and financial means that will permit them to create firms and, above all, to withstand victoriously both internal, as well as external, foreign competition.[75]

The Senegalization of the economy consisted in penetrating the higher circles of management, and in promoting the rise of a technostructure originating from the existing bourgeois cadres. The means to that end was an alliance between the state and the emerging Senegalese business class. Viewed thus, "there is a symbiotic relationship between the governmental superstructure and the national industrial technostructure. Beyond its traditional interventions in the regulation of the economy, the state has acquired the function of entrepreneur."[76] The state sought to create the necessary conditions for the Senegalization of the economy. This implied certain reforms in the industrial and banking systems. On the one hand, the state expanded its involvement in the economy by creating several public and mixed industrial firms that contributed to the rise of private and semiprivate Senegalese enterprises and, on the other, it took command of several banks to facilitate the extension of credits to the aspiring national bourgeoisie.[77]

Between 1970 and 1975, the state created seventy parastatal agencies to induce the participation of foreign investments in the development of industry, mining, and tourism. By 1975, the modern sector was increasingly controlled by these parastatals, which generated more than 40 percent of its value added and employed about a third of its total working force.[78] The transition to "statism" was facilitated by a favorable international conjuncture of extremely high world market prices for Senegal's two major exports, phosphates and peanuts.

Such favorable economic conjuncture helped also the process of democratization initiated by Senghor in 1974, with the legalization of Abdoulaye Wade's Parti démocratique sénégalais (PDS). The PDS originated from the demands of two hundred cadres for the abolition of the de facto one-party state and the development of a real democracy. These demands, contained in what was called the "Manifesto of the 200," were very similar to those elaborated by the CND.[79] In this perspective, the legalization of the PDS contributed to the rise of *l'opposition constructive*, which provided a useful outlet for a few segments of the frustrated and powerless intelligentsia. The PDS, however, because of its very moderation, could not contain the more radical challenges of clandestine left wing organizations. While it partly legitimated Senghor's regime, it failed to integrate these organizations into the existing structures of governance. The legalization of the PDS alone did not suffice; the passive revolution required the cooptation and absorption of both the moderate and the antagonistic opposition. Without such cooptation and absorption the passive revolution would have remained incomplete and dangerously weak; its success depended on whether Senghor's regime had the capacity and will to integrate its political enemies into reformed structures of governance.

Such integration, however, hinged upon the ruling class's understanding that its power and status were best preserved by the acceptance of certain sacrifices and the promotion of policies that went beyond its own narrow corporate interests. Accordingly, the passive revolution does not bring to the fore a radical restructuring of the political system and of the relationships between rulers and ruled; it merely legitimates and consolidates this system and these relationships by giving them a new appearance in a more liberal climate. Yet, it creates opportunities and challenges for both the ruling class and the opposition. In these conditions it is not surprising that Senghor imparted to the Senegalese passive revolution a gradual and moderate rhythm. As he explained in 1976:

> In both our politics and our political economy, we have been suspicious of romanticism and improvisations. We shall continue to advance, not slowly, but at a moderate pace. This is what we have been doing for the last sixteen years, while avoiding the shocks, especially the brutal stops and the steps backwards, which provoke disappointments and crises.[80]

Senghor's moderate course consisted in slowly integrating past political enemies into a gradually changing institutional framework. The legalization of the PDS in 1974 was followed by the constitutional revision of 1976, which transformed Senegal into a tripartite political system. The UPS became the Parti socialiste, and was legally forced to adhere to the doctrine of democratic socialism; the PDS had to espouse the modern liberal credo; and the Parti africain de l'indépendance had to embody the Marxist-Leninist ideology.[81] In 1979, a fourth party, the Mouvement républicain sénégalais representing the conservative current was legalized. By the end of the 1970s the political system was characterized by a limited pluralism that recognized what Senghor held to be the four most important Senegalese political families. This pluralism, however, was contested by different unrecognized movements that rejected the harsh constitutional and ideological constraints on the formation of political parties.[82]

Senghor's refusal to legalize unlimited pluralism generated a profound political alienation, which was exacerbated by the general economic crisis of the mid–1970s. Soaring oil bills, rising food imports, higher inflation rates, and a precipitous decline in the world market prices for Senegal's two major exports provoked a fiscal crisis in the state. In addition, the terrible and persistent drought aggravated the already precarious agricultural situation. The economic crisis had reached such egregious proportions that the World Bank estimated that the per capita income had decreased by 3 percent in the countryside and by 21 percent in the cities between 1964 and 1974.[83] The government sought to alleviate the crisis by increasing its external debt and by diversifying the financial, technological, and political sources of its dependence.[84] Such a strategy, however, left Senegal on the verge of total economic collapse and bankruptcy.

Senegal's debt at the end of the 1970s climbed to well over $1 billion, and servicing it represented more than 20 percent of exports. During the same decade, food imports amounted to an average of 20 billion francs CFA annually, and the oil bill increased from 2.5 billion francs CFA to 50 billion francs CFA in 1980.[85] Confronted with such astronomical expenses, the regime opted to come under the economic tutelage of the International Monetary Fund in 1979.[86] The tutelage facilitated the refinancing of the debt, but it called for a plan of economic recovery that necessitated the massive imposition of austerity.

After two decades of independence, Senghor's strategy of growth and development had failed miserably, it increased dependence on foreign sources of power, it generated the virtual bankruptcy of the state, and it did not improve markedly the standard of living of the vast majority. A new organic crisis was again threatening Senegalese society. It is in this climate of a collapsing economy, a decaying political situation, and a vanishing popularity that Senghor decided to resign the presidency on 31 December 1980. As provided by the constitution, Prime Minister Abdou Diouf assumed the presidency.

The Dioufist Period

Diouf moved rapidly to defuse the emerging organic crisis that he had inherited. Under his leadership, the national assembly legalized all political parties, irrespective of their ideology. The new president had realized that his contested legitimacy and the survival of the political system required a bold departure—the bringing in of unlimited pluralism was the means to that end. It represented the single most important formative effort of the ruling class, and it consolidated and certainly assured the relative success of the Senegalese passive revolution. Integrating the opposition into reformed structures of governance inevitably transformed it; from being a threat to the passive revolution, the opposition became the fulfillment of the passive revolution itself.   Jacques Mariel Nzouankeu explains that

> a limited multiparty system, however, had the inconvenience of ignoring political tendencies that identified themselves with the great currents of thought, but which sought to preserve their own originality and personality. Now, it is a sociological fact that when groups are not integrated in the political game they strive to organize their own game. This may prevent democracy from working properly. Moreover, it is difficult to measure the real influence of groups that evolve clandestinely, and it is possible to commit two errors in assessing their importance: their true representativeness may be underestimated or overestimated. In either case, such error in judgment distorts the rules of the political game.[87]

The introduction of unlimited pluralism absorbed the opposition into the constitutional forms of liberal parliamentarism, and integrated its demands into a systemic framework that secured the representation of ruling class interests. Under Diouf's leadership, the Senegalese passive revolution had reached its political limits; it contributed to the containment of the organic crisis and to the rise of a new social configuration and ideological discourse.

After a short period marked by a relative continuity with Senghor's political legacy, Diouf began to articulate his own themes and slogans.[88] As Diouf explained, if he was to be *l'homme de la fidelité*, he would also be *l'artisan du changement*:

> Admiration and fidelity are my feelings for my master. But, as he has taught me, the fidelity of the disciple and the inspiration of the master in no way destroy their respective personalities.
> The seed is planted.
> I will preserve continuity while introducing changes and maintaining what has already been accomplished.[89]

With his landslide victory in the presidential elections of 1983, Diouf's own themes and slogans acquired a new vigor, immediacy, and substance.[90] While Diouf proposed a politics of conciliation and national unity, he unequivocally asserted the primacy of the Parti socialiste. He invited the opposition to join the government in developing common responses to the fundamental problems facing the country.[91] He believed that a national consensus could be reached on matters related to the unity and integrity of the republic, to the secular nature of the state, and to the consolidation of democratic practices.[92] Such a consensus would lead to what Diouf called *le sursaut national*, the regeneration of the country. Diouf's general political report of January 1984 explains:

> It is not possible ... it is not conceivable, that a political formation, be it majoritarian, could ... develop an exclusivist conception of the Senegalese future by believing that it and only it could be the source of all that had to be undertaken and accomplished. We Senegalese Socialists have always known that we never retained the exclusivity on patriotism and nationalism. Being and remaining ourselves, that is to say profoundly Senegalese, we ought to demonstrate a spirit of openness in our reflection, generosity in our action, and thus accept the extended hand of others, especially when this gesture contributes to the strengthening of national unity and solidarity.[93]

This *ouverture* towards the opposition, however, never implied the sharing of governmental responsibilities; it merely indicated that Senegalese cadres of whatever political persuasion could, as individuals, join and support the Dioufist regime.[94] As the president himself put it, it was *l'ouverture, mais dans la fermeté*.[95] Not surprisingly, the vast majority of the opposition rejected these appeals as self-serving and meaningless. Several left wing parties joined in an informal alliance—the Front d'action anti-impérialiste, Suxxali reew mi—to put an end to what they described as the neocolonial *régime PS*.[96]

Diouf's appeals for a consensus, though, had some success with independent nationalist cadres. A new generation of organic intellectuals sought to give to the Diouf government a greater homogeneity and awareness of its own function in the economic, political, social, and ideological realms. These intellectuals strongly favored the development of an all-encompassing movement of national unity that would go beyond doctrinaire differences and personal animosities. In what became known as *l'appel des 1500*, an informal grouping of such intellectuals under the leadership of Iba Der Thiam called for

> all the active forces of the country [to] fully participate in the search and application of sure and efficient solutions to the

great national problems....

To be effective, however, such an undertaking requires from the involved parties four certainties:

1. The certainty that a party, whichever it might be, cannot by itself victoriously lead the fight against underdevelopment if it monopolizes power or if others only help it grudgingly
2. The certainty that no partisan grouping will possess by itself the monopoly over the truth, the whole truth
3. The certainty that the search for and the issuing of a *programme d'union, de salut et de renouveau national,* cannot succeed without mutual concessions and reciprocal renunciations
4. The certainty that unity, even if sought and achieved, is always consolidated by a program ... whose definition and fulfillment have depended on the individual and collective involvement of the contracting parties[97]

L'appel des 1500 expressed the organic intellectuals' desire for some form of government of national unity that would obtain the support of all major social forces. It strongly echoed Diouf's *sursaut national* and, to that extent, it represented more a demand for the internal democratization and opening of the PS than a serious and meaningful *ouverture* to the parties of the opposition. More plainly, the organic intellectuals were creating the terrain for their own entry into the avenues of power. Not surprisingly, they sought more structured means than the *appel des 1500* to voice their aspirations and goals. Regrouped in two new organizations, the Groupe de rencontres et d'échanges pour un sénégal nouveau (GRESEN) founded by Professor Amadou Booker Sadji and the Comité de soutien à l'action du président Abdou Diouf (COSAPAD), they attempted to forge a larger, broader, and new vision of society—a vision that would create the most favorable conditions for legitimating Diouf and the interests he represented. Although both GRESEN and COSAPAD had initially claimed a relative autonomy from the governing Parti socialiste, they gradually fused with it. In 1984, the most important members of GRESEN and the COSAPAD, as an organization, formally joined the PS.[98] GRESEN explained the fusion in the following way:

GRESEN,... identifying itself with President Abdou Diouf's policies of change, because they correspond to the interests of the Senegalese people, has deemed it necessary to support and accelerate their implementation....

At the same time ... the members of GRESEN ... have decided to bring their active, militant, and unified support to the work of change and renewal of President Abdou Diouf, by reconfirming their membership in the Parti socialiste, or by joining it as free individuals....[99]

In spite of their efforts, the organic intellectuals have not successfully transformed Diouf's themes of national consensus and *sursaut national* into a meaningful and popular political ideology. If Diouf had enjoyed the massive support of all Senegalese in the first three years of his presidency, his popularity had declined dramatically by 1985. In a poll conducted in February and March 1985 by the monthly *Liberté*, 50.8 percent of the population had a favorable impression of the president, while 43.4 reacted negatively to him. More significant, only 27.8 percent of the respondents believed that Diouf was the individual most capable of handling the economic and social crisis plaguing Senegal. Abdoulaye Wade, leader of the main opposition party, the Parti démocratique sénégalais, was a close second with 24.8 percent.[100] Whatever the statistical merits of the poll, it clearly indicated a precipitous decline in Diouf's popularity from the heyday of his electoral triumph with more than 80 percent of the vote. As Babacar Sine, the organic intellectual par excellence of Dioufism, explained in a 1984 article in the progovernment daily *Le Soleil*:

> Today, the period of the state of grace is over; it lasted two years, between January 1981 and August 1983.
>
> From now on, a new relationship exists between Diouf and the Senegalese people, a relationship based on truth.... This relationship deserves to be strengthened, because it conditions the support given by the people of Senegal to the chief of state and his government.... It is necessary, however, to inform national public opinion of the accomplishments and efforts of the government.... This is, in our opinion, the crux of the problem: to facilitate the accurate apprehension, perception, and understanding of presidential activity by a people who has already massively supported it in elections, but who has yet to be convinced of the pertinence of its policies.[101]

The declining popularity of Diouf represented, however, a more fundamental and multifaceted phenomenon than just a lack of effective ideological dissemination. It symbolized the virulence of the economic crisis and the profound cracks in the construction of an integral state in a peripheral nation like Senegal. While it is true that the social malaise engulfing the Senegalese polity is a function of the ruling class's weak ideological hegemony, this weakness, is in turn, the product of its extremely fragile and dependent material base. Such a fragile base has imparted to any hegemonic project clear and inflexible limitations. That a relatively successful passive revolution took place at all under these circumstances is a tribute to the political talents, sophistication, and maturity of the Senegalese ruling class. Their talents, however, should not mask the ruling class's incapacity to resolve the profound and persistent economic crisis.

The economic crisis of the 1980s is generalized: more than 70 percent of the potentially active urban population is unemployed, and, from 1980 to 1984, some seven thousand industrial workers lost their jobs. Inflation reached 30 percent in 1982 and continued to escalate in 1983 as a result of increases of 15 to 40 percent in the prices of rice, sugar, oil, water and electricity.[102]   Furthermore, Senegal's external debt was estimated to be close to 500 billion francs CFA in 1983. In 1981, the servicing of such massive debt represented 20 percent of the national budget and more than 25 percent of Senegal's total exports. The government had a total deficit of more than 100 billion francs CFA in 1982.[103] Not surprisingly, it is with dramatic language that the Senegalese intellectual Pathé Diagne describes his country's predicament:

> Senegal, in the 1980s, looks like a country just coming out of war. Its economy and society are in crisis. Its uprooted populations barely survive in the cities and villages. They are condemned to powerlessness in the face of an environment that has become hostile. Postcolonial Senegal is an enormous and artificial superstructure centered on Dakar....
>
> The Senegalese state, concentrated in Dakar, and manipulated by a vast technocracy, avoids ... bankruptcy ... thanks to a foreign assistance that undermines its independence.[104]

The economic crisis has contributed to Senegal's increasing dependence on foreign institutional forces and sources of finance. The nation's program of recovery responds more to the exogenous demands of organizations such as the International Monetary Fund (IMF) or the World Bank than to the domestic needs of the vast majority of its population.[105] The fundamental elements of the plan of recovery elaborated by the IMF and Diouf's government consist of curbing internal demand through a monetarist fiscal policy designed to limit credit and state expenditures. It is a program of austerity bent on forcing the Senegalese population to live and spend according to its modest means. It has exacerbated social tensions by disproportionately affecting the low- and middle-income sectors while leaving virtually untouched the ruling class regrouped in the state bureaucracy. Diagne remarks:

> With a budget of 275 billion [francs CFA], an elite monopolizes the state and its public firms control projects financed externally, as well as 40 to 60 percent of the real national income. The political and technocratic elite gets a large share of the state's taxes.
>
> Each of the 60,000 civil servants spends an annual average of 4 million [francs CFA] out of a national budget of 275 billion francs.... The standard of living of the state has not changed. Parliament, in 1983, increased its expenditures by raising the salaries and privileges of deputies and commission presidents....[106]

The IMF-inspired plan of austerity has reinforced social inequalities and failed to confront those dominant political forces that have a vested interest in the preservation of the status quo. The Diouf government has merely sought to manage and survive the crisis according to the orthodox monetarist guidelines of the IMF, and in the hope that a coming world economic recovery would usher in a new period of growth and prosperity.[107] By so doing, it has largely accepted the norms of the resurgent liberal free market ideology and begun to denationalize and privatize the economy. It has been forced to submit to the "recolonization of Africa."[108] As Isebill Gruhn, writing in 1983, explains:

> Now, in the 1980s a new form of external control and management has emerged. This latest colonization of Africa is by international bureaucracies....
>
> The IMF international teams of bureaucrats do not much resemble traditional colonizers or the salesmen from multinational corporations.... [The] IMF does not merely send out its medicine men in consultation teams. It has installed them in African banks and treasuries.... Options have shrunk along with reduced and declining resources. Today, a poor,

weak African state, rather than having too many options,
basically has only one: to accept, more or less, and seek to
implement whatever medicine is recommended by the IMF-
World Bank and to hope that bilateral, multilateral, public and
private additional assistance will flow as a consequence. It
means, in effect, opting into ... 'recolonization'....[109]

The government has justified this "recolonization" in the
name of greater productivity and efficiency: it is the means of
modernizing socialism itself. In his defense of this new
economic approach President Diouf suggested that

> one must not confuse socialization and statism. Admittedly, our
> socialist and democratic course is characterized by state
> intervention in key sectors of the economy. But its originality
> resides in its expressed desire to liberate individual energies and
> all initiatives so as to promote productivity and social justice....
> Through the privatization of certain public firms, we wanted to
> show that for us, socialism was not synonymous with bad
> management and bureaucracy. And that, indeed, socialism is
> synonymous with economic efficiency, competitiveness,
> productivity, and profitability.[110]

The adoption of free market policies under the strong urging
of the IMF, however defended, can only erode the already weak
socialist credentials of the Parti socialiste. This erosion has
contributed to a further loss in the regime's ideological
legitimacy and has thus created profound cracks in the
hegemonic projects of the ruling class. Moreover, the process of
privatization radically calls into question the earlier dominant
ideology that it is the technocratic state that ensures the general
welfare of the population. By doing so, it challenges the very
raison d'être of the vast bureaucratic apparatus. Such a
challenge exposes the state bureaucracy to the vicissitudes of
unemployment and decline, and it thus entails sapping the
political foundation on which rest the power and authority of the
PS regime. In other words, privatization implies the
debureaucratization of the state and the consequent threat to the
job security of civil servants who represent the social base of the
Diouf government. This means that the new laissez-faire
ideology is Janus-faced: it strengthens the regime to the extent
that it facilitates the necessary flow of foreign assistance, but it
simultaneously weakens the regime by eroding its bureaucratic
political support.

In this sense, the dependent, peripheral, and backward character of the Senegalese economy is now imposing obdurate limitations on the impressive work of the organic intellectuals and on the passive revolution itself. The formative efforts of the ruling class have been incapable of generating the ideological and material resources that the construction and consolidation of the integral state entailed. In the absence of strong ideological leadership and direction, and in the context of a resurging "soft" state, the hegemonic alternative may reside in Islam and its *marabout* representatives.[111]

Islam, as a total world view that answers the existential questions about the meaning of life, "explains" history, and imparts "true knowledge" to its believers, may become, in the context of a silent and persistent organic crisis, the national ideology of Senegal. Deeply rooted in popular tradition, it transcends class, ethnicity, and geography and it offers an alternative set of normative beliefs and practices to the dominant Western model. In these conditions, the *marabouts* and the different Islamic brotherhoods may embody the most effective organic intellectuals of Senegalese society. As Copans explains in *Les Marabouts de l'Arachide*:

> The universal vocation of Murid Islam manifests itself in a national ambition that goes beyond the confines of its geographical and class origins.... Its transethnic and transclass ideological content gives it an indubitable efficiency. Thus, without desiring it explicitly, the Murid brotherhood is capable of diffusing the only true national ideology. This possibility is the more likely because the Murid ideology is rooted, on the one hand, in the labor process and in relationships of production and expresses, on the other hand, a discourse and social practice that are free from imperialist domination....[112]

The development of Islam as the Senegalese national ideology is constrained, however, by its own doctrinal divisions between "reformists" and *marabouts,* and by the competitive drive of the different brotherhoods for new disciples.[113] The reformists who are more attached to the rigorous and textual interpretation of the Koran are opposed to what they perceive as the relative laxity and secularization of maraboutic Islam. This opposition, nurtured by the state, does not necessarily preclude an alliance and a compromise, but it makes more difficult the realization of any Islamic hegemonic project. In addition, the spread of a populist form of Islam, which neither the state nor the brotherhoods are likely to control, might inevitably increase social polarization and ultimately threaten the stability of the state and the position of the religious authorities themselves.   Given this possibility, both the government and the *marabouts* have a vested interest in moderating the hegemonic potentialities of Islam.   In these circumstances, the construction of an integral state, whether it be technocratic, nationalist, or Islamic is seriously constrained by the material, political, and cultural contradictions characterizing the structures of governance of the ruling class.

The limits to the formation of an integral state also indicate the limits to the work of the organic intellectuals.   The peripheral and dependent nature of the Senegalese economy and the entrenched interests of the ruling class set definite parameters to the reformist and nationalist projects of these intellectuals.   The vision of an integral state gradually dissipated in the face of the harsh economic and political realities of the 1980s: the state had to restrain its reach and could no longer pretend to be all-encompassing; and it could no longer be the central agent of material growth and the general provider of social benefits.   President Diouf explains:

> Now, more than ever, is the time to break with laxity, laziness, futility, the mentality of dependence, and the myth of the providential state.   It is therefore necessary to transform our social philosophy to celebrate work and not racketeering, responsibility and not Pontius Pilatism, personal and collective efforts and not systematic dependence on the state.   A new approach is required to give primacy to initiative, a sense of rigor, and self-sacrifice.[114]

What Diouf is calling into question is the organic intellectuals' project of an integral state capable of effectively intervening in the economy and society to promote material gains and social welfare.   The retreat to a less interventionist state was caused less by the fear of collectivism and bureaucratism than by the objective constraints of Senegal's peripheral and dependent capitalist economy.

It is these constraints that imposed serious limitations on the intellectuals' vision of an integral state.   This is not to say that Senegal's organic intellectuals are impotent managers of legitimation; their mental labor formulated, announced, and articulated the main contours of the passive revolution.   But it is precisely because organic intellectuals are managers of legitimation that their project could not go beyond existing socioeconomic structures and thus avoid the contradictions and limitations that such structures entailed. The difficulties involved in the creation of an integral state, however, reflect much more than the relative political failure of the intellectuals in implementing the totality of their projects and visions. To a considerable extent these difficulties are symptomatic of the enduring solidity of patron-client relationships.

These relationships are usually conceived of as symbols of a persistent "tradition" impinging on, and/or retarding the transition to "modernity." They are also presented as evidence of the limited theoretical and explanatory usefulness of class analysis. In the following chapter, I will seek to demonstrate that, while patron-client relationships impinge adversely on the rationalization and construction of an integral state, they nonetheless serve and protect the interests and dominance of the ruling class. They are a useful heuristic tool to understand Senegalese politics, but they are neither a substitute for class analysis nor are they to be construed as an independent paradigm of their own. They should be used as complementary, not contradictory, variables to class.

Notes

1. Ibrahima Fall, *Sous-Développement et Démocratie Multipartisane: L'Expérience Sénégalaise*, Dakar: Les Nouvelles Editions Africaines, 1977. Jacques Mariel Nzouankeu, *Les Partis Politiques Sénégalais*, Dakar: Editions Claireafrique, 1984. Donal B. Cruise O'Brien, "Senegal," in John Dunn, ed., *West African States: Failure and Promise*, Cambridge: Cambridge University Press, 1978, 173–188.

2. Anne Showstack Sassoon, "Passive Revolution and the Politics of Reform," in Anne Showstack Sassoon, ed., *Approaches to Gramsci*, London: Writers and Readers, 1982, 133.

3. Antonio Gramsci, *Selections From the Prison Notebooks*, edited and translated by Quintin Hoare and Geoffrey Nowell Smith, London: Lawrence and Wishart, 1971, 181.

4. I am indebted to my colleague Dante Germino for pointing out to me the intellectual connection between Gramsci and Cuoco on the issue of the passive revolution. See also Sassoon, "Passive Revolution and the Politics of Reform," 127–148.

5. Gramsci, *Selections from the Prison Notebooks*, 178.

6. Ibid., 177.

7. Stuart Hall, "Moving Right," *Socialist Review*, 55 (1981): 113–137.

8. Ibid., 117.

9. Ernesto Laclau and Chantal Mouffe, *Hegemony and Socialist Strategy*, London: Verso, 1985, 7.

10. Gramsci, *Selections from the Prison Notebooks*, 211.

11. Monique Anson-Meyer, *Mécanismes de l'Exploitation en Afrique. L'Exemple du Sénégal*, La Rochelle: Editions Cujas, 1974.

12. Guy Rocheteau, *Pouvoir Financier et Indépendance Economique en Afrique: Le Cas du Sénégal*, Paris: Karthala, 1982, 231–239.

13. N. Casswell, "Autopsie de l'ONCAD: La Politique Arachidière au Sénégal, 1966–1980," *Politique Africaine*, No. 14, (1984) 39–40, (my translation).

14. Ibid., 41.

15. Ibid., 41–42.

16. Ibid., 44. See also Paul Thibaud, "Document: Dia, Senghor et le Socialisme Africain," *Esprit*, No. 320, 332–348.

17. Gerti Hesseling, *Histoire Politique du Sénégal*, Paris: Karthala, 1985, 62.

18. Robert H. Bates, *Markets and States in Tropical Africa. The Political Basis of Agricultural Policies* , Berkeley: University of California Press, 1981, 30–44. Casswell, "Autopsie de l'ONCAD: La Politique Arachidière au Sénégal, 1966–1980," 63.

19. Casswell, "Autopsie de l'ONCAD: La Politique Arachidière au Sénégal, 1966–1980," 44 (my translation).

20. Ibid. Edward J. Schumacher, *Politics, Bureaucracy, and Rural Development in Senegal*, Berkeley: University of California Press, 1975, 160.

21. Schumacher, *Politics, Bureaucracy, and Rural Development in Senegal*, 182.

22. Ibid., 183.

23. Ibid., 184. Casswell, "Autopsie de l'ONCAD: La Politique Arachidière au Sénégal, 1966–1980," 47.

24. Casswell, "Autopsie de l'ONCAD: La Politique Arachidière au Sénégal, 1966–1980," 66–69. Christian Coulon, *Le Marabout et le Prince*, Paris: Editions A. Pedone, 1981, 240–243.

25. Coulon, *Le Marabout et le Prince*, 266 (my translation).

26. Schumacher, *Politics, Bureaucracy, and Rural Development in Senegal*, 184–185.

27. Ibid., 213–218; Casswell, "Autopsie de l'ONCAD: La Politique Arachidière au Sénégal, 1966–1980," 50.

28. Goran Hyden, *No Shortcuts to Progress,* Berkeley: University of California Press, 1983.

29. Casswell, "Autopsie de l'ONCAD: La Politique Arachidière au Sénégal, 1966–1980," 50, (my translation).

30. Ibid., 63.

31. Boubacar Barry, "Les Indépendances Africaines: Origines et Conséquences du Transfert du Pouvoir 1956–1980—Le Sénégal, 1960–1980," Colloqium, University of Zimbabwe, January 8–11, 1985. Ousman Blondin Diop, *Les Héritiers d'une Indépendance*, Dakar: Les Nouvelles Editions Africaines, 1982, 39–41. Hesseling, *Histoire Politique du Sénégal*, 261–263. Francis Mulot, "Syndicalisme et Politique au Sénégal (1968/69–1976)," *Revue Française d'Etudes Politiques Africaines*, No. 158, (1979): 63–90.

32. Pierre Biarnes, "Sénégal: Montée d'un Patronat Africain," *Revue Française d'Etudes Politiques Africaines*, No. 35, (1968): 14 (my translation).

33. Ibid., 15.

34. Ibid, 15–16. Rocheteau, *Pouvoir Financier et Indépendance Economique en Afrique: Le Cas du Sénégal*, 364.

35. Chris Gerry, "The Crisis of the Self–Employed: Petty Production and Capitalist Production in Dakar," in Rita Cruise O'Brien, ed., *The Political Economy of Underdevelopment: Dependence in Senegal*, Beverly Hills: Sage Publications, 1979, 131.

36. Rocheteau, *Pouvoir Financier et Indépendance Economique: Le Cas du Sénégal*, 364 (my translation).

37. Pierre Fougeyrollas, *Où Va le Sénégal?* Paris: Editions Anthropos, 1970, 12–15.

38. Hesseling, *Histoire Politique du Sénégal*, 262. Mulot, "Syndicalisme et Politique au Sénégal (1968/69–1976)," 66.

39. Coulon, *Le Marabout et le Prince*, 235. Hesseling, *Histoire Politique du Sénégal*, 263.

40. Barry, "Les Indépendances Africaines: Origines et Conséquences du Transfert du Pouvoir, 1965–1980—Le Sénégal, 1960–1980," 20.

41. Hesseling, *Histoire Politique du Sénégal*, 262. Mulot, "Syndicalisme et Politique au Sénégal (1968/69–1976)," 66.

42. Mulot, "Syndicalisme et Politique au Sénégal (1968/69–1976)," 66.

43. Ibid., 68–73.

44. Fougeyrollas, *Où Va le Sénégal?* 14–15 (my translation).

45. Gramsci, *Selections from the Prison Notebooks*, 210–211.

46. Ibid., 275–276.

47. Ibid., 5, 12.

48. Ibid., 181–182.

49. Senghor, as quoted in Irving Leonard Markovitz, *Léopold Sédar Senghor and the Politics of Négritude*, New York: Atheneum, 1969, 206.

50. Gilles Blanchet, *Elites et Changements en Afrique et au Sénégal*, Paris: ORSTOM, 1983, 140.

51. Ibid., 278.

52. Ibid., 209.

53. Club Nation et Développement du Sénégal, *Club Nation et Développement du Sénégal*, Paris: Présence Africaine, 1972, 7.

54. Ibid., 8. See also 12 (my translation).

55. Ibid., 17.

56. Ibid., 14.

57. Ibid., 18–20 (my translation).

58. Ibid., 21–127.

59. Ibid., 119 (my translation).

60. Ibid., 23 (my translation).

61. Léopold Sédar Senghor, *Rapport de Politique Générale: Le Plan du Décollage Economique ou la Participation Responsable Comme Moteur du Développement*, Dakar: Grande Imprimerie Africaine, 1972, 178 (my translation).

62. Gramsci, *Selections From the Prison Notebooks*, 222.

63. Club Nation et Développement, 22 (my translation).

64. Ibid., 77–78 (my translation).

65. Gramsci, *Selections from the Prison Notebooks*, 181–182.

66. As quoted in Mulot, "Syndicalisme et Politique au Sénégal (1968–69/1976)," 70 (my translation).

67. Senghor, *Rapport de Politique Générale*, 173 (my translation).

68. Jean Copans, *Les Marabouts de L'Arachide,* Paris: Le Sycomore, 1980, 249 (my translation).

69. Blanchet, *Elites et Changements en Afrique et au Sénégal*, 190–191, 327;Copans, *Les Marabouts de L'Arachide*, 248–249; Coulon, *Le Marabout et le Prince*, 289–295.

70. Hesseling, *Histoire Politique du Sénégal*, 262–270.

71. Blanchet, *Elites et Changements en Afrique et au Sénégal*, 189–190, 278.

72. Anson-Meyer, *Mécanismes de l'Exploitation en Afrique. L'Exemple du Sénégal*, 92–95. Blanchet, *Elites et Changements en Afrique et au Sénégal*, 327. Jean-Claude Gautron, "Les Entreprises Publiques, Acteur et Indicateur du Changement Social," *Revue Française d'Etudes Politiques Africaines*, 158, (1979): 54–62. Rocheteau, *Pouvoir Financier et Indépendance Economique en Afrique: Le Cas du Sénégal*, 365–377.

73. Senghor, *Rapport de Politique Générale*, 174–175, (my translation).

74. Ibid., 68.

75. Ibid., 71–72 (my translation).

76. Rocheteau, *Pouvoir Financier et Indépendance Economique en Afrique: Le Cas du Sénégal*, 375 (my translation).

77. Ibid., 368.

78. Sheldon Gellar, "The Politics of Accomodation: The Evolution of State-Society Relationships in Senegal in the Post-Colonial Era," Paper presented at the 27th Annual Meeting of the African Studies Association, Los Angeles, 1984, 24.

79. Christine Desouches, *Le Parti Démocratique Sénégalais*, Paris: Berger-Levrault, 1983, 23–27.

80. Léopold Sédar Senghor, *Pour une Société Sénégalaise Socialiste*

et Démocratique, Dakar: Les Nouvelles Editions Africaines, 1976, 11 (my translation).

81. Fall, *Sous-Développement et Démocratie Multipartisane: L'Expérience Sénégalaise*. Nzouankeu, *Les Partis Politiques Sénégalais*. O'Brien, "Senegal."

82. Hesseling, *Histoire Politique du Sénégal*, 270–285; Nzouankeu, *Les Partis Politiques Sénégalais*.

83. Hesseling, *Histoire Politique du Sénégal*, 74. Sheldon Gellar, *Senegal: An African Nation Between Islam and the West*, Boulder: Westview Press, 1982, 45–66.

84. Rocheteau, *Pouvoir Financier et Indépendance Economique en Afrique: Le Cas du Sénégal*, 369–377.

85. Pathé F. Diagne, *Sénégal: Crise Economique et Sociale et Devenir de la Démocratie*, Dakar: Sankore, 1984, 89–92. Gellar, *Senegal: An African Nation Between Islam and the West*, 52.

86. Isebill V. Gruhn, "The Recolonization of Africa: International Organizations on the March," *Africa Today*, Vol. 30, No. 4, (1983): 37–48.

87. Nzouankeu, *Les Partis Politiques Sénégalais*, 33 (my translation).

88. Hesseling, *Histoire Politique du Sénégal*, 288–292.

89. Abdou Diouf, *Le Sursaut National*, Dakar: Publications du Parti Socialiste, no date, 14–15 (my translation).

90. Abdou Diouf, *Rapport de Politique Générale: Le PS, Moteur du Sursaut National*, Dakar: Publications du Parti Socialiste, 1984. See also Jacques Mariel Nzouankeu, "L'Evolution des Partis Politiques Sénégalais depuis le 22 Juillet 1983," *Revue des Institutions Politiques et Administratives du Sénégal*, 8, (octobre–décembre 1983): 773–783.

91. Diouf, *Rapport de Politique Générale: Le PS, Moteur du Sursaut National*, 28–31.

92. Ibid., 29.

93. Ibid., 20 (my translation).

94. *Le Soleil*, April 29, 1985: 4.

95. Diouf, *Rapport de Politique Générale: Le PS, Moteur du Sursaut National*, 27.

96. Nzouankeu, "L'Evolution des Partis Politiques Sénégalais depuis le 22 Juillet 1983," 775, 784–785.

97. As quoted in *Revue des Institutions Politiques et Administratives du Sénégal*, No. 5, (octobre–décembre 1982): 873 (my translation).

98. Nzouankeu, "L'Evolution des Partis Politiques Sénégalais depuis le 22 Juillet 1983," 782.

99. As quoted in *Revue des Institutions Politiques et Administratives du Sénégal*, 8 (octobre–décembre 1983): 809–810 (my translation).

100. *Liberté*, March 1985: 12–17.

101. Babacar Sine, "Abdou Diouf entre Deux Fronts," *Le Soleil*, 20

Juillet 1984: 1–5 (my translation).

102. Diagne, *Sénégal: Crise Economique et Sociale et Devenir de la Démocratie*, 20–21.

103. Ibid., 91.

104. Ibid., 90–92 (my translation).

105. Ibid., 32–36.

106. Ibid., 21–22, 34 (my translation).

107. Ibid., 27.

108. Gruhn, "The Recolonization of Africa."

109. Ibid., 37–48.

110. Abdou Diouf, *Rapport Introductif*, Dakar: Conseil National du Parti Socialiste, 1985, 11–12 (my translation).

111. Copans, *Les Marabouts de l'Arachide*, 251–258. Coulon, *Le Marabout et le Prince*, 294–295.

112. Copans, *Les Marabouts de l'Arachide*, 256–257 (my translation).

113. Christian Coulon, *Les Musulmans et le Pouvoir en Afrique Noire* , Paris: Editions Karthala, 1983, 120–142. Lucy E. Creevey, "Muslim Brotherhoods and Politics in Senegal in 1985," *The Journal of Modern African Studies*, Vol. 23, No. 4 (1985): 715–721.

114. Abdou Diouf, *Le Sursaut National*, 90 (my translation).

4

The Integral State and Patron-Client Relationships

In this chapter I analyze how patron-client relationships have perpetuated traditional patterns of domination and subordination and contributed to weakening the processes of political democratization and bureaucratic rationalization that the passive revolution entailed. The passive revolution has not succeeded in eliminating patron-client relationships; and it could not succeed. Corresponding to a situation in which the ruling class "reabsorbs the control that was slipping from its grasp," it was bound to maintain those structures of power that preserved order and sustained the social continuity of life.[1] The success of the Senegalese passive revolution was largely dependent on the support of the *marabouts* and, thus, on their network of patronage, the source of their material power. While the passive revolution failed to suppress *la politique politicienne*, it created the emerging, if weak, structures of an integral state. The integral state is that state that is capable of establishing both the historical unity of the different factions of the ruling class and the proper "organic relations between ... political society and civil society."[2] The integral state expresses, therefore, the effective hegemonic capacity and repressive potential that the ruling class exercises over civil society and political society respectively.

The emerging Senegalese integral state is continually endangered by the persistence of patron-client relationships, which erode its effectiveness and authority. These relationships, however, are necessary if the democratization of Senegal is to remain within the confines of a passive revolution. Thus, patron-client relationships and the passive revolution appear as contrasting horns of a dilemma.

Patron-Client Relationships in Theoretical Perspective

The precolonial African culture of the Muslim brotherhoods along with the rather liberal electoral patterns established by French colonialism in the eighteenth century imparted to Senegal patron-client relationships that have permeated its politics since independence.[3] These relationships, which have been defined as pertaining to the transitional mode of behavior characteristic of modernizing societies, represent, in the eyes of many observers, one of the most serious roadblocks to Senegalese development.[4] In fact, former President Senghor lamented their corrupting impact on governmental life and came to define them as *la politique politicienne* or *la Sénégalite*, the national disease of Senegal.[5]

According to many analysts, however, *la politique politicienne* has many redeeming qualities. It assures a "respectably high degree of popular participation in politics, a circulation of political elites, and a wide, if not equitable, distribution of the spoils of political power."[6] From this perspective, it tends to diffuse social conflicts and social polarization and "to provide some of the basis for a viable polity...."[7] This is why these analysts claim that the class struggle is absent from Senegalese politics, or that it is completely obliterated by the personal alliances and animosities of the patron-client relationship. Indeed, the patron-client paradigm seeks to demonstrate that class analysis fails to capture the social reality of modernizing societies and, consequently, that it is of little relevance to their study. As James C. Scott puts it:

> By and large ... [the] overall value [of Marxist class theory] is dubious in the typical nonindustrial situation where most political groupings cut vertically across class lines and where even nominally class-based organizations like trade unions operate within parochial boundaries of ethnicity or religion or are simply personal vehicles. In a wider sense, too, the fact that class categories are not prominent in either oral or written political discourse in the Third World damages their a priori explanatory value.[8]

This perspective, however, is quite mistaken. The existence and persistence of patron-client relationships should not be perceived as a substitute for and/or a destroyer of class conflicts, but rather as a supplement and indeed a supporter of class rule.[9] In the Senegalese case, the patron-client relationship has reinforced the existing structures of wealth and privilege. By blurring and making more bearable class exploitation, the personal character of the patron-client relationship has served the interests of the ruling class. Class power became, as it were, invisible and thus the most effective and pervasive. This is what Samuel Huntington has called, in another context, the "power paradox: ... effective power is unnoticed power; power observed is power devalued.... The architects of power ... must create a force that can be felt but not seen. Power remains strong when it remains in the dark; exposed to the sunlight it begins to evaporate."[10] What is important, however, for our immediate purposes is to clarify and explain in more detail the concept of patronage and clientelism, and to study its implications for Senegal.

As defined by Scott, patron-client relationships represent inegalitarian patterns of exchange that are marked by a certain reciprocity and affection rather than domination and exploitation, and by personal and diffuse linkages rather than class power and control.[11] They embody the essence of politics in nonindustrial and agrarian societies, and they are a resilient structure that constrains "modernizers" to neotraditional values and modes of behavior. Accordingly, patron-client relationships block the ascendancy of rational forms of organization and prevent the imposition of developmental macroeconomic policies. In sum, they limit the scope and effectiveness of the managers of the state. Simultaneously, however, they mitigate the devastating effects of industrialization, urbanization, and proletarianization. They are the vehicle of a less painful transition to modernity, and they offer to the traditional and bewildered masses a heaven in a heartless world. They provide an "exit" from unpopular governmental demands and a "voice" to modify these very demands.[12]

Patron-client relationships symbolize, therefore, the relative powerlessness of national leaders and political-administrative institutions in modernizing societies. This is why Zolberg has claimed that the central paradox of African politics reflects the fact that "the party-state is authoritarian within its domain, but that at the same time this domain is very limited, and that on the whole the regime has little authority."[13] The inevitable result is that governmental policies favoring modernization will founder on the inertia of the traditional sector and will be circumscribed by the personalistic and ascriptive web of patron-client relationships.

It is from this perspective that many observers have explained the persistent stagnation of the Senegalese economy and the countless failures of bureaucratic reforms. Edward J. Schumacher states that

> the limited effectiveness of the governing elite's endeavors during the first decade of independence points to a dilemma that no doubt will continue to confront Senegalese leaders for some time to come: namely, the very resilience of political clientelism, especially in its machine form, constitutes one of the most entrenched obstacles facing the leadership's effort to transform the state bureaucracy into the system of development administration deemed necessary for attaining the regime's basic economic objectives.... One likely response to this dilemma may well entail the incremental attenuation of initial development goals, the pursuit of economic growth devoid of any vision of fundamental change in socioeconomic relationships and values, and thus the reorientation of public policy toward the efficient management, and perpetuation, of the status quo.[14]

What Schumacher and the view that he espouses fail to appreciate is that the leadership is not truly confronting a dilemma, since it has always benefited from and actively participated in patron-client relationships. This is not to say that the modernizers see these relationships as the best possible structure of social organization and development; on the contrary, they are bent on constituting a strong state that would directly control and ultimately dissolve these very relationships. The modernizers, however, know that their objective class interests are best served by the maintenance of the existing patterns of wealth and power and, consequently, of the patron-client relationships. Indeed, these relationships have dissipated and defused the general crisis and discontent generated by the failures of Senegalese peripheral capitalism. In this sense, patron-client relationships are more instruments of class control and means of disorganizing subaltern classes than ties of affection and reciprocity.

It is, therefore, not surprising to discover that the sites of modernity, namely the bureaucratic apparatus and the dominant political party have been permeated by the politics of clientelism. Schumacher himself recognizes that

> [the party] since its initial victories in the early fifties has deeply marked the administrative process in Senegal by politicizing both the recruitment, promotion, posting, and disciplining of civil service personnel and the local administration and use of other administrative resources.... [It has played a] decisive role in instilling and sustaining clientelistic norms and behavior within the state bureaucracy....[15]

In fact, the more the state and the party penetrated society the more they enhanced the value of clientelism and patronage.[16] The modernizing bureaucrats sought to take over and manipulate to their own advantage the existing political system, rather than create autonomous bases of power for radical social change. Theirs was not a strategy of socialist reconstruction and popular empowerment, but one of accommodation with and acceptance of the traditional conservative classes.[17] In its undertaking of drastically restructuring the allocation of wealth and power, the ruling bureaucratic stratum of the Senegalese state was forced to rely on local notables and patrons to pursue its politics of moderate and gradual change. As a result, "influentials" have illicitly acquired public resources for their own private, materialistic interests; governmental institutions have been transformed into arenas of struggles over the distribution of spoils, jobs and promotion; and politics has become a cynical exchange of favors.[18]

Such a politics has inevitably fragmented the Senegalese ruling class into clans and factions. These divisions, however, are certainly not fundamental; neither are they primarily based on principles or ideology, although they may appear to be; they are, in fact, rooted in the struggle over scarce material resources. It is true that such a struggle expresses also a certain ethical search for status as *samba linguer* or "first among the nobles," but ultimately it is the expanded acquisition of money that guarantees success, honor, and, most importantly, a large clientele. As Foltz has argued, the patron "must have and distribute money ... [and] since the financial rewards of politics are likely to be considerable, it may well be necessary for an aspiring *samba linguer* to try his fortune in the political arena.... [Indeed] the prime reason for anyone's going into politics is to make money."[19]

Although it is true that the patron's appropriation of wealth may reflect his desire to provide for his clientele's subsistence, it embodies also his self-interested search for financial aggrandizement. Thus, inasmuch as patron-client politics rests on the unequal acquisition and sharing of material rewards and payoffs, it is embedded in unlawful and illicit practices. This, in turn, stifles the civic culture, corrupts public life, and engenders a pervasive political cynicism. As clientelism displaces any notion of the common good and functions as a means of enrichment for the Senegalese ruling class, politics inevitably becomes a struggle between competing factions and clans over scarce resources, thereby breeding corruption and nepotism.[20] Also, by preserving the ties of dependence between the upper and lower classes, and by blocking the ascendancy of class consciousness, the clientelist system cements the structures of domination and exploitation. Indeed, it contributes to the fact that the peasantry and proletariat experience their subjection not as organized classes, but as individuals enmeshed in highly personalist and parochial relations. Moreover, it freezes the profoundly unequal distribution of resources by legitimizing the patrons' extraction of the economic surplus from their clients' labor. Stated plainly, the clientelist system inexorably implies the existence of a small ruling class capable of obtaining and controlling the resources produced by the masses; it is inherently hierarchic, exploitative, and corrupt.

It is true that the patron-client relationship involves a certain reciprocity, but it is a deeply flawed reciprocity that tends to benefit the patron. By virtue of his monopolistic or oligopolistic control over scarce and vital resources, the patron can unilaterally command the obedience of those whose very survival depends on their access to such resources.[21] Still, the profound inequality that patron-client relationships entail has to rest on a legitimating evocation of meanings if clients are to remain quiescent or supportive; and, in turn, such evocation of meanings must be rooted in a certain material reality. In fact, it expresses the patron's capacity to both deliver needed services and critical resources to his clientele and protect it effectively from the excessive reach and demands of higher authorities. The patron must have, or at least must be seen to have, a relative autonomy from the state if he is to defend the particular interests of his clientele. In Senegal, the *marabouts* or heads of the major Islamic brotherhoods have enjoyed such an autonomy, and it is to them that we turn our attention in the next section.

Patron-Client Relationships and the
Relative Autonomy of Maraboutic Power

The importance and influence of the *marabouts* and their brotherhoods in Senegalese politics cannot be overlooked.[22] In a country where Muslims represent 85 to 90 percent of the 5.5 million population, their impact can be decisive. These *marabouts* and brotherhoods have always played a significant role in Senegalese history. During the era of colonial conquest, they represented a *contre société* resisting the implantation of alien forces. Once colonialism firmly established its roots, however, they accommodated themselves to the colonial authorities and eventually became powerful economic and political forces. On the one hand, they functioned as intermediaries between the colonial administration and their peasant disciples or *taalibes*; on the other, they emerged as significant material agents engaged in the production of peanut, which had and still has a determining impact on Senegal's economy.

The *marabouts'* intermediary position between the "center" of power and the "*taalibe* periphery" reflected the contradictory nature of their loyalties and experiences. In certain fundamental ways, they provided a moral and religious community, as well as valuable protection and assistance to the Muslim peasantry. The *marabouts* were enmeshed in a patron-client relationship whereby, as patrons, they extended to their peasant clients the material and spiritual support of belonging to a prestigious Islamic brotherhood. In return, the *marabouts* expected the devotion, allegiance, and free labor of their clients.[23] But the *marabouts'* reliance on the center for resources and power limited their autonomy and much of their potential contribution to the peasant periphery; the *marabouts*, paradoxically, themselves became the clients of the patron colonial state. To this extent, they assumed the role of accommodationists, but they were accommodationists with a difference: they enjoyed a systematic hold over their mass peasant following, and as such, they retained a certain degree of independence from their colonial patrons from which they exacted concessions.

The contradictory position and accommodationist role of the

marabouts has survived colonialism and has continued to shape the politics of independent Senegal. The economic dominance of the *marabouts* over the cultivation of peanut has inextricably forced the postcolonial state to furnish the religious authorities with the necessary productive and marketing infrastructure. This economic dominance of the *marabouts* stems from the significant material contributions that the *taalibes* provide them. The *taalibes'* religious convictions and submission are therefore transformed into the material gains of the *marabouts*.

The *taalibes*, who are poor peasants, give 10 percent of their harvest to their *marabout*; in addition, they offer him their free labor to cultivate his fields. But it is because they perceive him as an intermediary of God that they consent to such sacrifices; the *taalibes* are convinced that the *marabout* is blessed with divine powers and virtues from which stem his *baraka* ("luck") and charisma.[24]

The *marabouts'* charismatic hold on their peasant clients, however, derives not merely from religious beliefs and subordination; it is decisively dependent on the state's material largesse.[25] The *marabouts'* power has traditionally been associated with their capacity to attract the recognition and contributions of the established political order without becoming its subservient instrument—the more the *marabout* is effective at reconciling these two conflicting objectives, the more he can project his *baraka* into patronage and influence. Accordingly, the state and the *marabouts* are involved in mutually supportive and beneficial relations.

These relations characterize also the political domain. Here again, the *marabouts* perform an intermediary role similar to the one they exercised in colonial times. They represent a transmission belt between the urban center and the agricultural periphery; they help the state penetrate the countryside, but, in return, they mold that penetration and indeed manipulate it to their own advantages. To be effective political intermediaries, the *marabouts* must continuously act or at least pretend to act independently from the state; they cannot afford to be identified as the mere instruments and representatives of the ruling political class. Their legitimacy as spiritual and moral patrons of the peasant *taalibe* relies on their capacity to be perceived as the sacred symbol of protection from and opposition to the state.

This perception expresses a real fact: namely, that the *marabouts*, by their very nature as intermediaries, must extend their protection and assistance to their disciples even if this contradicts their symbiotic relationship with the state. It is precisely such protection and assistance that enhances their political position vis-à-vis both the center and the periphery. This protection and assistance, however, is contained within definite bounds that are quite compatible with the existing social order and the center's political supremacy. It is a form of protection and assistance derived from accommodationism and not from a determined resistance to the state and its rulers, let alone from a revolutionary consciousness. Therefore, to use Coulon's apt phraseology, the *marabouts* embody a class of *courtiers politiques* engaged in permanent negotiations of dependence and authority with their patron state and peasant clientele.[26]

Not surprisingly, the *marabouts'* behavior reflects their ambivalent location in the political system. Christian Coulon tells us that

> the political talent of the *marabouts* consists of playing on the ambiguity of their political position: on the one hand, they use the resources the state provides them, on the other hand, they establish their distances from the state itself. The balance will move according to the political conjuncture. In a period of normalcy, or in a case of limited crisis, the *marabouts* will collaborate with the state. However, if the crisis is more profound, if popular discontent develops, especially in the rural milieu, the *marabouts* will become more critical of the regime without rejecting it totally. And if, in such a context, a few *marabouts* persist in supporting the government, they may risk their authority since, in the history of Senegalese political culture, the *marabouts* have always performed as a protection against oppressive power.[27]

It is in light of these facts that one must understand the malaise that characterized the relationship between the *marabouts* and the state during the last years of Senghor's regime. The massive economic crisis that plagued agriculture, and peanut cultivation in particular, heavily strained the Senghor-*marabout* axis. The price of peanut determined by the state marketing agency (ONCAD) was too low—in circumstances of food shortages, poor rainfalls, and rising domestic inflation—to stimulate peasant production. The profits ONCAD derived from its imposition of unequal, and indeed exploitative, terms of trade between the peasant periphery and the urban privileged bureaucratic center ushered in the *malaise paysan* that contributed to the relative deterioration of the alliance between Senghor and the brotherhoods.[28]

Abdou Lahatte Mbacke, the *khalifa-général* of the Murid brotherhood (to which more than half of peanut producers are affiliated), expressed his sympathy for a systematic peasant withdrawal to subsistence agriculture since peanut cultivation implied a material dependence on the state, which violated the injunctions of the *Koran* against indebtedness. Such strong defense of peasant interests against the excessive economic claims of the state has led Donal Cruise O'Brien to describe the brotherhood as "Africa's first autonomous peasant trade union."[29] While O'Brien's description is a clear exaggeration of the brotherhood's independence, it is nonetheless true that the government yielded and doubled the producer price in the face of a potentially crippling "peasant strike." It could not have done otherwise, since peanut products accounted for 40 to 50 percent of Senegalese exports and were therefore vital to the survival of the economy itself.

The government's concession, however, did not eliminate the increasing difficulties plaguing its relations with the brotherhoods. For it was not only the peanut question and the *malaise paysan* that contributed to these difficulties; there was also the Muslim dissatisfaction with both the Senghor-inspired *Code de la famille* adopted in 1972 and the increasingly secular behavior of the urban ruling class. On the one hand, the code was a direct challenge to the *marabouts'* control over legal matters in the periphery, since it suppressed the diversity of customary law with a single national legal structure.[30] On the other hand, the *marabouts* condemned the secularization and westernization of the governmental ruling class, which represented in their eyes a proof of corruption and a threat to Islam. Not surprisingly, Mbacke declared: "We Murids are in a compound, our lives governed by the teachings of [the founder] Amadou Bamba, by work and by prayer. Outside our compound we see nothing but Satan and all his works."[31]

This context explains the *marabouts'* less than overwhelming and unenthusiastic support for Senghor and his Parti socialiste during the general elections of 1978.[32] This marked a significant departure from the early days of independence when maraboutic power decisively contributed to Senghor's political victory over his main challenger, then Prime Minister Mamadou Dia.[33]

Thus, historically, the *marabouts'* capacity to influence the making of politics in Senegal has been decisive; in such circumstances, the premium for acquiring their support is high and extremely valuable for any aspiring politician. Moreover, because of their mass following they constitute an even more formidable political resource in an open electoral system. It is not difficult, then, to understand the significance of the overwhelming maraboutic support for the new President Abdou Diouf in the elections of 1983, and the opposition's simultaneous and contradictory attempt to Islamize its message, on the one hand, and to demystify maraboutic power, on the other.[34]

The *marabouts'* support for Diouf not only symbolized their allegiance to the first Muslim president of Senegal, it reflected also their faith in Diouf's victory and subsequent capacity to deliver the material resources so badly needed in the rural periphery. Supporting Diouf symbolized two mutually reinforcing strategies, one based on the fervor of Islamic religiosity and the other on the prudence of worldly politics.

The opposition, which consisted of fourteen parties[35] (eight of which competed in the legislative and four in the presidential elections), represented the center and Marxian left and, as such, it confronted maraboutic charges of atheism and materialistic corruption.[36] Resenting these charges and maraboutic support for Diouf, the opposition condemned the Islamic leaders' "lack of integrity, and corrupt spirit."[37] Further, it decried the partisan intrusion of Islam into politics and called for the neutrality of the brotherhoods during the elections. This, however, did not prevent the opposition from using Islamic symbols for its own purposes.[38] The point here is the significance of Muslim religion in Senegalese politics, even if the confrontation between *marabouts* and the parties of the opposition contributed to the relative demythologization of saintly power. Indeed, an important segment of the Murids rejected their khalifa's *ndiggal*, or religiously invoked command, to vote for Diouf.[39]

In this perspective, the relative erosion of maraboutic power may have reflected a certain conjunctural and very temporary decline in the electoral influence of patron-client relationships in Senegalese politics. It may also have indicated that, under the weight of the opposition's antimaraboutic charges, the peasantry came to reject slowly and hesitantly the ugly reality of subordination and injustices that these relationships entailed. The following section is an analysis of this reality of subordination and injustices.

The Reality of Patron-Client Relationships

Patron-client relationships reflect great inequalities of exchange and thoroughly lopsided structures of power, and, as such, they entail bonds of coercive dependence rather than ties of genuine reciprocity. Coercive dependence, however, does not entail or necessarily call forth the consciousness of suffering or exploitation or a sense of moral outrage. Patron-client relationships have, in fact, routinized and indeed legitimated coercive dependence by projecting it as a form of benevolent paternalism; they have established the moral authority of obedience and stifled the sense of injustice.[40] They have frozen the emergence of class conflict and enshrined as natural the existing hierarchy of domination and subordination. Coercive dependence has yet to generate massive popular resistance, but it is an objective reality.

In this perspective, Laura Guasti's conceptualization of clientelism in "misdeveloped" or "peripheral" societies will serve as a heuristic guide to our understanding of Senegalese politics. Guasti defines clientelism as

> a political structure whose basis is a highly unequal distribution of resources within society, and whose functioning serves to maintain the dependency of each class on those above it. Fundamentally, it is characterized by the patron-client relationship ... which, besides being based on an unequal holding of resources, is dyadic ... and flexibly diffuse in the types of resources that can be exchanged between the patron and client. The patron-client relationship is thus an unequal exchange of resources across class lines on an individualized basis. The relationship tends to maintain the lower class client in his dependent position vis-à-vis the higher-class patron because the client is more in need of the resources the patron monopolizes than the patron is in need of the resources the client offers. The client therefore can afford much less to terminate the exchange than the patron can. However, the commercial value of the resources given by all the clients of one patron to that patron is greater than the commercial value of the resources given by the patron to all his clients, and so the clientelistic, patron-centered group serves to funnel clients' surplus to the patron.[41]

Patron-client relationships are therefore processes of resource extraction and capital accumulation. In this sense, their economic structures and paternalistic ethos strengthen and enhance the material and political power of the patrons. They simultaneously disorganize and individualize the resistance and struggles of the clientele against its bonds of coercive dependence. Hence, patron/client relationships contribute to the transformation of patron authority into class authority, and they repress the collective challenge of subaltern classes.[42] As such, they are means of political control and financial aggrandizement.

In this sense, clientelism persists not so much because of the "traditionalism" of the Senegalese masses, but rather because its continued presence reinforces the power of the ruling groups. Indeed, the rhetorical commitment of these groups to the socialist transformation of the consciousness of the popular classes cannot crystallize as a living practice, since it would undermine the patron-client relationship which serves their objective interests. In other words, the relatively peaceful extraction of the economic surplus from the Senegalese masses for the benefits of a privileged and small state bureaucracy is founded on the maintenance of the personal and individual bonds of dependence that clientelism entails and nurtures.

One of the fundamental characteristics of patron-client relationships is that, in its actual practice, political domination fails to take the form of coercive bonds of exploitation between ruling and subordinate classes. It is as if class conflicts were nonexistent. This is so because patron-client relationships prevent the political organization of subordinate classes as classes, by maintaining and accentuating their isolation and individualization. On the other hand, they unify the dominant classes by linking them into a framework of cooperation closely associated to the state. In this sense, patron-client relationships integrate the patrons into, and exclude the clients from, the centers of national power. Clients are therefore personally dependent upon members of the dominant classes for their very survival; they receive petty favors for obedience and, in the process, are ultimately isolated from their own wider class as atomistic individuals who defer to local displays of wealth and power. Thus, patron-client relationships undermine solidarity among the oppressed by ligating them as individuals to their oppressors; clients are hard put to identify with each other as a class, and tend to behave as individuals incapable of cohering their grievances into collective resistance.

In this context, if patron-client relationships express the persistence of tradition, it is a tradition that is not only compatible with the rule of a modern state-technocracy, but it also enhances such a rule. Coulon maintains:

> The adoption by the 'traditionalist' masses of a new mentality and their insertion into the modern political system could undermine the hegemony of the urban political-bureaucratic class [and its 'intermediaries of the bush'] and endanger the revenues that it extracts from peasant labor.... By mobilizing the population on a terrain that is not a true battlefield because it is confined to quarrels between individuals, the patrons erect a protective screen between the ruling class and those on whose labor it lives. In such a context, it is difficult for the peasantry to become a class for itself. Clientelism and factional confrontations are thus no longer the residue of a traditional political culture, nor the political art of a modernizing society. They constitute hegemonic apparatuses ... that is to say, civil society's institutions of social control of the subaltern classes.[43]

Thus, while patron-client relationships express certain factional divisions within the ruling class, these divisions are contained within a common framework of understanding and interests. They stem from the personal animosities generated by both the struggle over scarce resources and the building of popular followings, rather than from principled political options and commitments. As Richard Sandbrook said: "Factionalism is a form of conflict over access to wealth, power, and status, frequently with only minor ideological and policy implications in which members of the conflict units are recruited on the basis of mercenary ties."[44]

In addition, factionalism is inherently unstable as clients are always prepared to shift their allegiances to the highest bidder and to the patron best suited to defend their collective and individual interests.[45] Accordingly, clients are continuously calculating which patrons are most effective in representing their demands and in articulating their grievances, and, in turn, patrons are permanently struggling for the influence and means necessary to maintain and expand their following.[46] However, this pattern of shifting alliances reflects more the reality of urban and "secular" politics than the nature of the *marabouts'* hold over the peasant *taalibes*. Indeed, since the patron-client relationship dominating the peripheral agricultural sector is profoundly imbued with Islamic fervor, it possesses a spiritual and religious dimension that imparts to it a relative stability and resistance to change.[47] Because its bonds of dependence are more ideological than opportunistic, and more spiritual than materialistic, the *marabouts'* clientele is less mercenary than its urban counterpart.

In the urban or central areas, loyalties rest on self-interest, not on the principles of the collective good. In these circumstances, the competition for power breeds nepotism and corruption at the highest political levels.[48] A widespread cynicism undermines developmental goals and makes a mockery of the leadership's demands for hard work and sacrifices. As Colin Leys has argued, the problem with corruption is that "to the extent that the official public morality of a society is more or less systematically subverted, especially if the leadership is involved in it, it becomes useless as a tool for getting things done, and this is expensive in any society where resources are scarce."[49] The result is the unethical and factional quest for acquiring and monopolizing the vital administrative resources of the state. Finally, the state itself becomes the superpatron of society, or, to put it more precisely, its top bureaucratic managers are the ultimate and decisive builders of clienteles.

As builders of clienteles, the managers of the state can develop political bases and control the regional and sectorial allocation of resources; such control confers on them the capacity to penetrate, at least indirectly, the peripheral areas of society. However, the penetration can hardly be rationalized since it is mediated by local notables who depend on patronage itself to maintain their status and wield effective authority.[50] Not surprisingly, therefore, the consolidation of state power is constrained by the rigid limitations of peripheral clientelism and by the necessity of strengthening this very periphery to counterbalance urban unrest and disaffection. As Clement Cottingham explains:

> A basic element in the central party elite's strategy for managing rising urban pressures consists of efforts aimed at enlarging the scope of rural support, while simultaneously exerting central administrative pressure to check monopolistic tendencies of local party elites. Since rural party elites must function in more traditional settings, they are little disposed to observe the bureaucratic norms currently emphasized by the UPS governing elite. In fact, for them to observe bureaucratic

norms would tend to reduce their local effectiveness in mobilizing support for the central government. Therefore, the UPS elite may find it necessary to loosen the enforcement of bureaucratic procedures in local society in order to mobilize additional political support for rural party elites.[51]

In this sense, the conflicts between the modernizers of the center and the traditionalists of the periphery tend to lose their intensity since they are completely subordinated to the imperatives of political stability and order. Moreover, the traditionalists are not necessarily threatened by the implantation of a new mode of governance; in fact, they have always manipulated such implantation by inserting it into their own modified structure of dominance. Accordingly, the traditionalists are not inherently opposed to change; what they seek is to direct and control it in the interest of consolidating and expanding their own privileged position. They form, therefore, a conservative class that knows that "modernizing tradition" preserves the economic and political system that sustains its power.[52] To this extent, there is a certain symbiotic relationship between central and peripheral ruling classes even if their objectives and policies differ in some instances.[53] Indeed, this symbiotic relationship crystallizes the unity of a single Senegalese ruling class.

Thus, patron-client relationships link central and peripheral ruling classes and reinforce the existing structures of power. Finally, they are also a manifestation of the patterns of dependence and misdevelopment characterizing the world capitalist economy; they represent the internal mode of capital appropriation and political control of the weak and disadvantaged peripheral ruling classes. The linkages of dependence and relative subservience to external forces from which these classes derive part of their power are reproduced locally to preserve the highly unequal access to wealth and prestige.[54] The domination of external forces in peripheral societies is mediated through a structure of superordination and subordination embodied in patron-client relationships. In other words, the bonds between external and internal forces constitute a complex whole reflecting not only the reality of the center's exploitation of the periphery, but also the coincidence of interests between ruling classes of both center and periphery.

Such coincidence of interests should not be surprising since it is rooted in what may be called the cross-national "instrumental friendship" of ruling patrons.   In this friendship, each patron promotes the interests of the other even if some patrons are clearly more equal than others.   The crucial question for the friendship is not whether it is thoroughly reciprocal, but whether it maintains the structures of the status quo at the national and international levels.   As Guasti argues:

> The highest-level patrons within the [peripheral] society depend, for both their access to and control over important resources in the society, on their unequal relationships with foreign capitalists, who control or have influence over the use of greater resources than do the highest-level patrons of the misdeveloped society. The patrons also depend on the maintenance of the disadvantaged international market position of their society, from which these relationships derive. The entire system of clientelistic networks within a society rests on the existence of unequal concentrations and control of resources. These occur from the lowest level of the misdeveloped society to the international market, where the society holds a disadvantaged position because international resource concentrations and control are held within the dominant capitalist societies.[55]

Participation in the world economy implies, however, the rationalization and modernization of patron-client relationships as a means to adapt old political structures to the new requirements of capitalist penetration.   This rationalization and modernization is the subject of the following section.

The Rationalization of Patron-Client Relationships

The processes and patterns of Senegal's dependent insertion in the world economy have contributed to the search for a rationalization of patron-client relationships.   The politics of administrative developmentalism that came to dominate the Senegalese governmental mode in the early 1970s, with the coming to power of young technocrats, reflected the adoption of an industrial strategy based on export-promotion rather than internal consumption.[56]   The resulting association between state and foreign capital required a more "rational bureaucratic" political structure.   In other words, patron-client relationships had to be modernized in order to support effectively the penetration of external economic forces and institutions.[57]

This is why a new politics of credits and a new philosophy of development had to be devised. As Guy Rocheteau, a former economic adviser to the Senegalese government, put it: "The objective is to select an entrepreuneurial elite capable of adapting itself to the requirements of modern management. From now on, the modernization of men is the sine qua non of industrial modernization."[58]

This new policy of *la modernisation des hommes*, initiated in 1969, forced the state to effect a centralization of clientelistic networks as a means of expanding its control over them and thus maximize its extraction of the domestic economic surplus. This process of centralization expressed the slow and uneven process of transformation of the soft Senegalese state into an integral state. The integral state represents the development of a technocratic undercurrent bent on managing and penetrating the domestic political economy, in close cooperation with transnational agencies and foreign capital.[59] This technocratic undercurrent favors the direct intervention of the state into the peripheral sectors of society. Rocheteau observes that

> as far as means are concerned, the fundamentally new element is the expansion of the economic responsibilities of the state that assumes—in the name of the nation, and in totally different conditions from those that characterized the industrialization of advanced countries—all the roles of the capitalist entrepreuneur.[60]

Not surprisingly, patron-client relationships had to be remodeled to conform to the new objectives of an expansionist state. In the words of Jonathan Barker:

> The new politics of administrative developmentalism is the only way the state managers can approach the urgent problems of a weak economy and they are reinforced in this approach by numerous transnational development agencies.... The trends have been to formalize and to contain factional politics within a neo-liberal economic system of expanding and centralizing state control of economic and administrative power, all in the name of progressive reform. As a direct result of these trends, the sheer size of the state apparatus has grown much faster than either population or production and considerably faster than the operating budget. [61]

Be that as it may, the bureaucratization of the Senegalese

state contributed to the institutionalization of a technocratic ideology based on the supremacy of "scientific" criteria of development. Indeed, by the late 1960s and early 1970s President Senghor's mounting fascination for technology and instrumental rationality imparted to the Senegalese political economy an increasingly bureaucratic character personified in then Prime Minister and future President Abdou Diouf.[62] Planning and the social control of growth were hailed as the master key to wealth and, ultimately, to the triumph of socialist *négritude*.[63] For Senghor, the problem of underdevelopment was to be resolved by the adoption of rational methods of production based on the efficacy of "the most modern scientific and technological discoveries, in sum on rationality." "Rationality [however, added Senghor] is not truth, which is the domain of philosophy, but efficiency, which is essential for underdeveloped countries. It is a question of an instrumental rationality and technology."[64]

In the eyes of both Senghor and his bureaucratic entourage, the instrumental rationality that planning embodied had little to do with political or ideological options; it was nothing but a "neutral" and scientific rationalization of the economic system. Planning, according to Senghor, represented

> a balanced ensemble of objectives and means which aims for a certain economic and social growth. It is a question of obtaining within a determined time and sector a calculated quantity of goods and services; agricultural and industrial products, schools and hospitals, housing and clothing, etc....[65]

It is not surprising that this political discourse and understanding of science have facilitated the penetration of transnational economic forces in Senegal. These forces, after all, represent the agents of modernity and thus they are to be welcome as tools of development yielding increasing quantities of wealth.[66] Put another way, the technocratic ideology has served to legitimate the alliance between the managers of the state and foreign capital.[67] This alliance, however, has not fostered the development of a "bureaucratic authoritarian" or "exclusionary corporatist" regime.[68] Rather, instead of contributing to the exclusion of popular sectors and organs, the construction of the Senegalese integral state has enhanced the participation of these sectors and organs by incorporating them into new liberal political structures.

As the preceding chapters have demonstrated, the legalization of a tripartite political system in 1976, under the impulsion of then President Senghor, marked the beginning of the passive revolution that President Diouf completed in 1981 with the creation of a liberal democracy and the legalization of all political parties.[69] This passive revolution, as I have argued, was the means to defuse the social, economic, and political crisis that undermined Senghor's and Diouf's regimes. It partially restored the legitimacy of the governing class at the internal and external levels, and it divided the opposition—especially the left—through the legalization of its competing factions and parties.[70] Moreover, after the long period of authoritarian presidentialism during which the structures of dependent capitalist (under)development had been firmly rooted, force and repression had become less necessary and, indeed, counterproductive.[71] The ushering in of liberal democracy reflected both the opposition's integration into these powerful structures of dependence, and the displacement of authoritarianism and force by a liberal "hegemony."[72] Since the Senegalese form of dependent capitalism had been firmly consolidated during the 1960s and mid-1970s, the relinquishment of authoritarianism for liberal democracy would hardly threaten the existing structure of power, wealth, and privilege. Liberal democracy was thus compatible with the interests of the ruling class.

Senegal's process of liberalization responded also to external pressures. In particular, Senghor's wish to integrate the UPS into the Socialist International required the establishment of a liberal democracy. As Senghor acknowledged, the admission of the UPS to that organization in late 1976 as the Parti socialiste (PS) was retarded because "the African socialist parties, even those claiming to embody the spirit of the Second International, had created in their respective countries single-party regimes—at least de facto ones."[73] In this perspective, the process of democratization expressed the cross-national instrumental friendship between the Senegalese ruling class and its powerful external patrons. This friendship was not only rooted in ideological ties of affection, it was also the means of gaining Senegal's preferential incorporation into the European capitalist network. In other words, the Senegalese ruling class sought to use its membership in the Socialist International and its new status as a liberal democracy to bargain for a less exploitative and less unequal relationship with international capital.[74]

Be that as it may, the structures of Senegalese dependent capitalism are rather unique in Africa, and the Third World in general, since they created the terrain for the implantation of a liberal democracy instead of the customary repression of military dictatorships and one-party states. Thus, only three of the four fundamental elements identified by O'Donnell as characterizing "bureaucratic authoritarianism" are present in Senegal. These elements are: "The reconstitution of mechanisms of capital accumulation in favour of large public and private organisations; ... the emergence of a new coalition whose principal members are state personnel,... international capital, and the segments of the local bourgeoisie which control the largest and most dynamic national business; and ... the expansion of the state; [these elements have not been accompanied by] the exclusion of a previously politically activated popular sector."[75] Seen this way, the Senegalese state embodies the structures of a "bureaucratic liberalism" rather than those of a bureaucratic authoritarianism; whereas it regulates and controls society, this state is more interventionist than coercive, more integrative than exclusionary, and more cooptative than repressive.

The Senegalese political phenomenon exhibits patterns and processes strikingly similar to what Gramsci termed the *trasformismo* of the Italian Risorgimento.[76] *Trasformismo*, as Adamson remarks, symbolizes "the predominance of political society over civil society in such a way that the subaltern classes are held in a passive position because their potential leadership is co-opted."[77] This cooptation can take a "molecular" or integral form. Molecular *trasformismo* is the process whereby "individual political figures formed by the democratic opposition parties are incorporated individually into the conservative-moderate 'political class.'" Integral *trasformismo* refers to the "transformism of entire groups of leftists who pass over to the moderate camp."[78]

In Senegal, molecular *trasformismo* occurred during the 1960s when individual leaders of the legal opposition disbanded their own parties and organs to join the UPS (Union progressiste sénégalaise) as cabinet members and/or deputies. In other words, the opposition was suppressed not so much because of repression, although that did exist, but rather because its major figures were absorbed in Senghor's regime as individual persons and not as representatives of parties. The Senegalese form of molecular *trasformismo* has been explained by Senghor himself:

> We have always 'recuperated' the dissidents. This is why I effected several political mergers in spite of the opposing opinions of my entourage.... Those who had ambitions, those who wanted to become ministers, transformed themselves into dissidents and formed a political party with which to bargain their integration into the governing party.... [Since] the French revolution, the Senegalese have quickly learned *la politique politicienne*.[79]

Senegalese molecular *trasformismo* was, therefore, a personalistic political process symbolizing the Machiavellian attributes of Senghor and the opportunistic character of the leaders of the opposition; in addition, it legitimated the notion of *parti unifié*.

The *parti unifié* differs theoretically from the *parti unique*, or single-party state, insofar as it results not from the suppression and elimination of all opposition, but from the political integration of such opposition, and to the extent that it tolerates, at least temporarily, the constitutionality of other parties. It is a form of coordinated coalitions between different social forces. It seeks to establish a centripetal political equilibrium between different parties within the united framework of a one-party state. Hence, theoretically, the *parti unifié* creates unity in diversity as it maintains a certain degree of internal, as well as external, pluralism.

In reality, however, the *parti unifié* has functioned very much like a one-party state with the significant exeption that it has suppressed the opposition with less violence and brutality. Cooptation rather than annihilation, subordination rather than destruction, and foreign exile rather than sudden death are its favored means of governance. Such means personified Senghor's understanding of the role of the opposition. For him the opposition, if it had to exist at all, had to be "constructive" and not "systematic." Indeed, it had to accept nothing else than the very supremacy and hegemony of Senghorism. As Senghor put it, "The opposition must pursue the same goal as the majority party. This is to prevent social groups from hardening into antagonist classes. Its role is precisely to be the conscience of government and majority parties."[80]

For Senghor, therefore, it was only logical that any conscientious opposition would ultimately fuse with the ruling party since, by definition, such opposition had to accept the ideological and programmatic approach of the government. As he explained in *The Road to African Socialism*, the UPS would never "despair of rallying the opposition to our national ideal.... Because our positions are just, we can rally the opposition to them."[81] It was in this context that Senghor's dream of a *parti unifié* finally materialized in 1966 when the Parti du rassemblement africain (PRA) merged with the UPS.[82] This merger, however, represented more the opportunistic nature of Senegalese molecular *trasformismo* than any principled ideological agreement. As O'Brien remarked in his analysis of the Senegalese opposition of the 1960s:

> If one must admire the tactical skill of President Senghor, one must also express some doubts as to the depth of commitment of most of the opposition.... Many who have joined the governing party have done so purely in order to enjoy the fruits of government, and are committed to no programme other than their own advancement. Those who have more widely ranging political preferences do not agree among themselves.
>
> The political machinery of the UPS does not provoke any overall unity. The party remains a coalition of notables, each with his private following, and little attempt is made to enforce discipline as long as nominal allegiance is given vociferously, and open opposition to government directives is avoided. The UPS provides a general framework within which clan struggles can be carried out; it does not provide a dynamic form of government.[83]

Thus, the Senegalese form of molecular *trasformismo* represented the notables' use of their popular clientele as a means to form parties and bargain for individual access to positions of power within Senghor's regime. Not surprisingly, molecular *trasformismo* contributed to the segmentation and disintegration of the UPS into a multiplicity of personal clans and cliques, turning it into the prime arena of *la politique politicienne* and of patron-client relationships. This resulted in the relative crisis of governance that severely constrained the capacity of the state to rule effectively. The absorption of the opposition into the UPS dispersed authority and blocked the successful implementation of macroeconomic policies. Again, O'Brien's observations on the politics of the 1960s capture well the essence of this crisis of governance:

> Opposition now is expressed more within the UPS than outside

it. Those parties which once existed as electoral machines now exist as clans or caucuses within the government. These groups continue to meet informally, and each retains a separate identity, despite verbal commitment to party unity: they are often divided into clans and sub-clans, the personal following of each leader. President Senghor has not succeeded in building a unified political party, or indeed in giving his party any particular sense of purpose. The party is not unified by any doctrine: while the President may have one, the various notables of the party diverge from it in different directions.[84]

It is not too surprising that these circumstances contributed to the general political and economic malaise of the late 1960s which profoundly rocked Senghor's regime. This malaise generated the organic crisis of the Senegalese state and, in turn, the development of what Stuart Hall has called, in a different context, the "formative strategy" of the ruling class.[85] On the one hand, the strategy was bent on rationalizing patron-client relationships within the structures of a technocratic and integral state; on the other, it sought to transform molecular *trasformismo* into an integral *trasformismo* whereby the opposition would be absorbed and co-opted into the existing system of power, no longer as individual notables, but as legal political parties. The emergence of a tripartite democracy became the means to that end and the basis for a new hegemony.[86] The political parties that the constitution of 1976 legalized represented to a large extent those clans and factions that had failed to gain ascendancy and influence within the UPS itself. Their incapacity to acquire and distribute the internal resources of patronage impelled them to move out of the UPS and set their own political organs and groups.[87]

To this extent, the institutionalization of tripartism in 1976 constituted an attempt to modify and restructure patron-client relationships; indeed, the legalization of the Parti démocratique sénégalais (PDS) expressed Senghor's desire to cure the political system from *la Sénégalite*. As Senghor himself explains:

> [By accepting] pluralism, I had wanted to stop the little games of
> *la politique politicienne*, [in accordance with which] ... from time
> to time, a member of the UPS would form a dissident party and
> wait until we came to plead for his return. Each time, ... I went to
> talk to the dissident to bring him back to the fold by

promising him a share of ministerial positions.... This is why, when members of the PRA-Sénégal, led by Abdoulaye Ly and Assane Seck, came back to the UPS, we decided that from then on we would no longer accept summit negotiations with the dissidents, and that those who wanted to join or return to the UPS would have to gain readmittance through the rank and file. This is why, when Abdoulaye Wade asked me in 1974 whether he could form a new party, I felt blackmailed and I said 'Yes': this is how the Parti démocratique du Sénégal was founded.[88]

Senghor's tripartite reform, however, eliminated neither the forces of clientelism that have traditionally pervaded Senegalese society, nor did they contribute to the eradication of the personal conflicts that have always characterized the governing party. On the contrary, these conflicts intensified in the late 1970s when Senghor's succession became the source of a major power struggle between the "barons" who initiated, dominated, and benefited from *la politique politicienne* from the very first days of independence, and the "young Turks" who had gradually come to occupy important positions in the technical sectors of the administration since the early 1970s. The coming to power of Diouf in 1981 and the subsequent ushering in of a multiparty liberal democracy signaled the defeat of the barons, but it did not end the sectional strifes that had traditionally divided the PS. As Diouf recognized:

Unfortunately, the quarrels of clans and political tendencies have too often turned our militants away from their essential duty. From now on, the confrontation of ideas will have to supercede the confrontation of people organized in competing clans. The real struggle has to be waged at this level—ideas and not clans have to gain primacy; this will contribute to the progress of our party....[89]

Such pronouncements, however, remained fruitless as *la politique politicienne* continued to dominate the internal affairs of the PS. In fact, the divisions of the PS reached such egregious proportions that Diouf was compelled to create in 1984 a Commission nationale des conflits, which would be empowered to impose order and unity in the party.[90] So far, however, the commission has failed to eliminate these sectional and personalistic confrontations. A clearly exasperated Diouf strongly condemned them at a special seminar of the central committee of the PS:

The personalization of politics at the grass roots for the conquest
or maintenance of local or national power proves that, in the
party, there only exist clans founded on groupings of people
swept along by the demons of electoralism, division, and
clientelism. The *claniques* become deaf to all *hierarchy of
interests*, even if their political discourse commits them
theoretically to defend, above all else, the interest of the party and
the nation. It is a sad sight that we contemplate in the structures
affected by the virus: 'freezing' of the minority or majority, or
both at once; blind monopolization of responsibilities, without
concern for their execution; electoralism, disrespect for the
instructions of the party; perversion through money;
government of one tendency due to the voluntary absence of the
other, etc.... Furthermore, the party, by devoting nearly all its
time to the arbitration of conflicts, has failed to concentrate on its
primordial tasks of educating the militants.[91]

It is no surprise that President Diouf expressed the ironic
sentiment that being general secretary of the Parti socialiste
was more complicated and difficult than being president.[92]
While the strong presidentialism of the Senegalese political
system implied that he was always the "majority" in his
government, the diffuse and clientelist nature of the Parti
socialiste's structures imposed certain limitations to his
decision-making power.

The persistence of clientelism within the ruling Parti
socialiste is a clear indication that the patterns of political and
material inequalities, giving rise to the phenomenon of
clientelism itself, have not been eradicated by the establishment
of liberal democratic processes. Really, patron-client relationships are more a symbol of great asymmetries of power, wealth,
and privilege than of "traditionality." Until these asymmetries
are radically altered in the direction of greater social justice
and equalities, the perverse effects of clientelism are unlikely to
disappear.

Thus, while the passive revolution has democratized the
political structures of Senegal, it has failed to create a climate of
social justice and harmony. This bodes poorly for the future of
far-reaching economic transformations in the direction of
greater chances for equality in life. The possibility of such
transformations is the subject of the next chapter, which seeks to
analyze critically the programs and policies of both the current
government and the opposition.

Notes

1. Antonio Gramsci, *Selections from Prison Notebooks*, London: Lawrence and Wishart, 1971, 210.
2. Ibid., 52.
3. Wesley G. Johnson, *The Emergence of Black Politics in Senegal* , Stanford: Stanford University Press, 1971. Edward J. Schumacher, *Politics, Bureaucracy, and Rural Development in Senegal* , Berkeley: University of California Press, 1975.
4. Jonathan Barker, "Political Factionalism in Senegal," *Canadian Journal of African Studies*, Vol. 7, No. 2, (1973): 287–303. Clement Cottingham, "Political Consolidation and Centre-Local Relations in Senegal," *Canadian Journal of African Studies*, Vol. 4, No. 1, (1970): 101–120. William J. Foltz, "Social Structure and Political Behavior of Senegalese Elites," in Steffen W. Schmidt et al., eds., *Friends, Followers and Factions*, Berkeley: University of California Press, 1977, 242–250. René Lemarchand, "Political Clientelism and Ethnicity in Tropical Africa," in Steffen W. Schmidt et al., eds., *Friends, Followers and Factions*, Berkeley: University of California Press, 1977, 100–123. Donal B. Cruise O'Brien, *Saints and Politicians*, Cambridge: Cambridge University Press, 1975. Schumacher, *Politics, Bureaucracy, and Rural Development in Senegal.*
5. Léopold Sédar Senghor, *Léopold Sédar Senghor: La Poésie de l'Action: Conversations avec Mohamed Aziza,* Paris: Stock, 1980, 174, 224–225.
6. Foltz, "Social Structure and Political Behavior of Senegalese Elites," 248.
7. O'Brien, *Saints and Politicians,* 177.
8. James C. Scott, "Patron-Client Politics and Political Change in Southeast Asia," in Steffen W. Schmidt et al., eds., *Friends, Followers, and Factions*, Berkeley: University of California Press, 1977, 123.
9. Jean Copans, "Paysannerie et Politique au Sénégal," *Cahiers d'Etudes Africaines*, No. 69–70, (1978): 241–256; *Les Marabouts de l'Arachide*, Paris: Le Sycomore, 1980. Christian Coulon, "Elections, Factions et Idéologie au Sénégal," in Centre d'Etude d'Afrique Noire ed., *Aux Urnes l'Afrique! Elections et Pouvoirs en Afrique Noire*, Paris: Editions A. Pedone, 1978, 149–186. P. Flynn, "Class, Clientelism and Coercion: Some Mechanisms of Internal Dependency and Control," *Journal of Commonwealth Political Studies*, Vol. 12, No. 2, (1974): 133–156. Laura Guasti, "Peru: Clientelism and Internal Control," in Steffen W. Schmidt et al., eds., *Friends, Followers, and Factions,* Berkeley: University of California Press, 1977, 422–438. Richard Sandbrook, "Patrons, Clients, and Factions: New Dimensions of Conflict Analysis in Africa," *Canadian Journal of Political Science*, Vol. 5, No. 1, (1972): 104–119.
10. Samuel P. Huntington, *American Politics: The Promise of Disharmony*, Cambridge: Harvard University Press, 1981, 75.

11. Scott, "Patron-Client Politics and Political Change in Southeast Asia," 125–126.

12. Albert Hirschman, *Essays in Trespassing: Economics to Politics and Beyond*, Cambridge: Cambridge University Press, 1981, 211–265.

13. Aristide Zolberg, *Creating Political Order*, Chicago: Rand McNally, 1966, 134.

14. Schumacher, *Politics, Bureaucracy, and Rural Development in Senegal*, 228.

15. Ibid., 226.

16. Coulon, "Elections, Factions et Idéologies au Sénégal."

17. Irving Leonard Markovitz, "Traditional Social Structure, the Islamic Brotherhoods, and Political Development in Senegal," *The Journal of Modern African Studies*, Vol. 8, No. 1, (1970): 73–96.

18. O'Brien, *Saints and Politicians*, 187–200.

19. Foltz, "Social Structure and Political Behavior of Senegalese Elites," 243–245.

20. Copans, "Paysannerie et Politique au Sénégal," 247–248.

21. James Scott and Benedict J. Kerkvliet, "How Traditional Rural Patrons Lose Legitimacy: A Theory with Special Reference to Southeast Asia," in Steffen W. Schmidt et al., eds., *Friends, Followers and Factions* , Berkeley: University of California Press, 1977, 442.

22. Lucy Behrman, *Muslim Brotherhoods and Politics in Senegal*, Cambridge: Harvard University Press, 1970. Copans, *Les Marabouts de l'Arachide*. Christian Coulon, *Le Marabout et le Prince*, Paris: Editions A. Pedone, 1980. Donal B. Cruise O'Brien, *The Mourides of Senegal* , Oxford: Oxford University Press, 1971; *Saints and Politicians*.

23. Abdoulaye-Bara Diop, *La Société Wolof*, Paris: Karthala, 1981, 297–319. Foltz, "Social Structure and Political Behavior of Senegalese Elites." Lemarchand, "Political Clientelism and Ethnicity in Tropical Africa."

24. Christian Coulon, "Les Marabouts Idéologiques," *Politique Africaine*, No. 4, (1981): 107–108.

25. Copans, "Paysannerie et Politique au Sénégal." Christian Coulon, "Les Marabouts Sénégalais et l'Etat," *Revue Française de Politiques Africaines*, No. 158, (1979): 15–42.

26. Ibid., 20.

27. Ibid., 37 (my translation).

28. Donal Cruise O'Brien, "Ruling Class and Peasantry in Senegal, 1960–1976: The Politics of a Monocrop Economy," in Rita Cruise O'Brien, ed., *The Political Economy of Underdevelopment: Dependence in Senegal*, Beverly Hills: Sage Publications, 1979, 219–220. André Terrisse, "Aspects du Malaise Paysan au Sénégal," *Revue Française d'Etudes Politiques Africaines*, No. 55, (1970): 79–91.

29. O'Brien, "Ruling Class and Peasantry in Senegal, 1960–1976: The Politics of a Monocrop Economy," 222–226.

30. Coulon, "Les Marabouts Sénégalais et l'Etat," 40.

31. O'Brien, "Ruling Class and Peasantry in Senegal, 1960–1976: The Politics of a Monocrop Economy," 222.

32. Coulon, "Les Marabouts Sénégalais et l'Etat," 38.

33. O'Brien, *The Mourides of Senegal*, 274–275.

34. Donal Cruise O'Brien, "Les Elections Sénégalaises du 27 Février 1983," *Politique Africaine*, No. 14, (1983): 11–12. *West Africa*, 21 February 1983: 460–461.

35. *Le Soleil*, 9 janvier 1983: 1; 28 février, 1983: 1–23. Jacques Mariel Nzouankeu, "L'Evolution des Partis Politiques Sénégalais Depuis le 22 Juillet 1983," *Revue des Institutions Politiques et Administratives du Sénégal*, No. 8, (1983): 773–783.

36. *West Africa*, 14 March 1983: 644.

37. Ibid.

38. Ibid., 644–645.

39. O'Brien, "Les Elections Sénégalaises du 27 Février 1983," 11–12.

40. Barrington Moore, Jr., *Injustice: The Social Bases of Obedience and Revolt*, White Plains, N.Y.: M.E. Sharpe, 1978.

41. Guasti, "Peru: Clientelism and Internal Control," 423.

42. Coulon, "Elections, Factions et Idéologies au Sénégal," 183.

43. Ibid., 182–183 (my translation).

44. Sandbrook, "Patrons, Clients, and Factions: New Dimensions of Conflict Analysis in Africa," 115.

45. O'Brien, *Saints and Politicians*, 152–164.

46. Sandbrook, "Patrons, Clients, and Factions: New Dimensions of Conflict Analysis in Africa," 113.

47. Coulon, "Elections, Factions et Idéologies au Sénégal," 156–157. Diop, *La Société Wolof*, 297–319. Foltz, "Social Structure and Political Behavior of Senegalese Elites."

48. O'Brien, *Saints and Politicians*, 187–200.

49. Colin Leys, "What is the Problem About Corruption?" *The Journal of Modern African Studies*, Vol. 3, No. 2, (1965): 228.

50. Christian Coulon, "Pouvoir Oligarchique et Mutations Sociales et Politiques au Fouta-Toro," in Jean-Louis Balans et al., eds., *Autonomie Locale et Intégration Nationale au Sénégal*, Paris: Editions A. Pedone, 1975, 23–80.

51. Cottingham, "Political Consolidation and Centre-Local Relations in Senegal," 103–104.

52. Markovitz, "Traditional Social Structure, The Islamic Brotherhoods, and Political Development in Senegal," 93–96.

53. Coulon, "Pouvoir Oligarchique et Mutations Sociales et Politiques au Fouta-Toro," 80.

54. Samir Amin, *Neo-Colonialism in West Africa*, Harmondsworth: Penguin Books, 1973. Abdoulaye Ly, *L'Emergence du Néocolonialisme au Sénégal*, Dakar: Editions Xamle, 1981.

55. Guasti, "Peru: Clientelism and Internal Control," 423–424.

56. Lapido Adamolekun, "Bureaucrats and the Senegalese Political

Process," *The Journal of Modern African Studies*, Vol. 9, No. 4, (1971): 555–556. Gilles Blanchet, "L'Evolution des Dirigeants Sénégalais de l'Indépendance à 1975," *Cahiers d'Etudes Africaines*, No. 69–70, (1978): 70–71; Guy Rocheteau, *Pouvoir Financier et Indépendance Economique en Afrique: Le Cas du Sénégal*, Paris: Karthala, 1982.

57. Rocheteau, *Pouvoir Financier et Indépendance Economique en Afrique: Le Cas du Sénégal*, 373–375.

58. Ibid., 365.

59. Ibid., 365–377. See also Schumacher, *Politics, Bureaucracy, and Rural Development in Senegal*, 213.

60. Rocheteau, *Pouvoir Financier et Indépendance Economique en Afrique: Le Cas du Sénégal*, 365 (my translation).

61. Jonathan Barker, "Stability and Stagnation: The State in Senegal," *Canadian Journal of African Studies*, Vol. 2, No. 1, (1977): 36–37.

62. Pierre Biarnes, "Sénégal: Les Jeunes au Pouvoir," *Revue Française d'Etudes Politiques Africaines*, No. 5, (1970): 9–11. Gilles Blanchet, *Elites et Changements en Afrique et au Sénégal*, Paris: ORSTOM, 1983, 190–191. Schumacher, *Politics, Bureaucracy, and Rural Development in Senegal*, 83.

63. Irving Leonard Markovitz, *Léopold Sédar Senghor and the Politics of Négritude*, New York: Atheneum, 29, 71, 165, 212–237.

64. Cited as quoted in Ibid., 71.

65. Ibid., 166.

66. Blanchet, "L'Evolution des Dirigeants Sénégalais de l'Indépendance à 1975," 71–72.

67. Rocheteau, *Pouvoir Financier et Indépendance Economique en Afrique: Le Cas du Sénégal*, 365–377.

68. Fernando Henrique Cardoso, "On the Characterization of Authoritarian Regimes in Latin America," in David Collier, ed., *The New Authoritarianism in Latin America*, Princeton: Princeton University Press, 1979, 33–57. David Collier, "Overview of the Bureaucratic-Authoritarian Model," in David Collier, ed., *The New Authoritarianism in Latin America*, Princeton: Princeton University Press, 1979, 19–32. Guillermo O'Donnell, "Tensions in the Bureaucratic-Authoritarian State and the Question of Democracy," in David Collier, ed., *The New Authoritarianism in Latin America*, Princeton: Princeton University Press, 1979, 285–318. Timothy Shaw, "Beyond Neocolonialism: Varieties of Corporatism in Africa," *The Journal of Modern African Studies*, Vol. 20, No. 2, (1982): 239–261.

69. Jacques Mariel Nzouankeu, *Les Partis Politiques Sénégalais* , Dakar: Editions Claireafrique, 1984.

70. Donal B. Cruise O'Brien, "Senegal," in John Dunn, ed., *West African States: Failure and Promise*, Cambridge: Cambridge University Press, 1978, 179.

71. Amin, *Neo-Colonialism in West Africa*. Ly, *L'Emergence du Néocolonialisme au Sénégal*. O'Brien, "Ruling Class and Peasantry

in Senegal, 1960–1976: The Politics of a Monocrop Economy."

72. Gramsci, *Selections From Prison Notebooks*, 206–276.

73. Senghor, *Léopold Sédar Senghor: La Poésie de l'Action: Conversations avec Mohamed Aziza*, 313–314 (my translation).

74. Rocheteau, *Pouvoir Financier et Indépendance Economique en Afrique: Le Cas du Sénégal*, 370–371.

75. O'Donnell, "Tensions in the Bureaucratic-Authoritarian State and the Question of Democracy," 78.

76. Gramsci, *Selections From Prison Notebooks*, 58, 109, 227.

77. Walter Adamson, *Hegemony and Revolution*, Berkeley: University of California Press, 1980, 175.

78. Gramsci, *Selections From Prison Notebooks*, 58 f.

79. Senghor, *Léopold Sédar Senghor: La Poésie de l'Action. Conversations Avec Mohamed Aziza*, 174 (my translation).

80. As quoted in Markovitz, *Léopold Sédar Senghor and the Politics of Négritude*, 199.

81. Ibid., 199–200 (my translation).

82. François Zuccarelli, *Un Parti Politique Africain: L'Union Progressiste Sénégalaise*, Paris: Pichon et Durand-Auzias, 1970, 94–103.

83. Donal B. Cruise O'Brien, "Political Opposition in Senegal: 1960–67," *Government and Opposition*, Vol. 2, No. 4, (1967): 564–566.

84. Ibid., 565.

85. Stuart Hall, "Moving Right," *Socialist Review*, No. 55, (1981): 113–137.

86. Ibrahima Fall, *Sous-Développement et Démocratie Multipartisane: L'Expérience Sénégalaise*, Dakar: Les Nouvelles Editions Africaines, 1977. Jacques Mariel Nzouankeu, *Les Partis Politiques Sénégalais*. François Zuccarelli, "L'Evolution Réçente de la Vie Politique au Sénégal," *Revue Française d'Etudes Politiques Africaines*, No. 127, (1976): 85–102.

87. Coulon, "Elections, Factions et Idéologies au Sénégal," 172–173.

88. Senghor, *Léopold Sédar Senghor: La Poésie de l'Action. Conversations avec Mohamed Aziza*, 224 (my translation).

89. Abdou Diouf, *Le Sursaut National avec Abdou Diouf*, Dakar: Publications du Parti Socialiste, no date, 31–32 (my translation).

90. Abdou Diouf, *Rapport de Politique Générale: Le PS, Moteur du Sursaut National*, Dakar: Publications du Parti Socialiste, 1984, 44–46.

91. Abdou Diouf, *Allocution d'Ouverture, Séminaire d'Etudes et de Recherches du Comité Central du Parti Socialiste*, Dakar: 1984, 4–5 (my translation).

92. Personal interview with President Diouf, November 8, 1985, Dakar.

5

Programs, Policies,
and the Transformation of
Senegalese Society

This chapter analyzes the ideological inclinations and the strategic aims of the governing Parti socialiste and the opposition. It studies also their understanding of the present as a means of exploring both their programmatic vision of the future, and their capacity to decisively influence it.

The Parti Socialiste (PS) and the *Sursaut National*

The introduction of unlimited multipartism under the leadership of Diouf created the terrain for the ideological and political remolding of the Parti socialiste. In Diouf's view, the PS had to democratize its internal structures, abolish the tradition of *la politique politicienne*, and establish the basis for a national consensus. The realization of these objectives would guarantee the continued supremacy of the PS and provide the foundation for the *sursaut national*—the revitalization of the nation.

Diouf called for the renewal and reinvigoration of the PS at its extraordinary congress of January 1984:

> I believe it is necessary to rethink our positions so as to improve the current policies of our party. I must emphasize, however, that this constitutes in no way an ideological reorientation, even less a questioning of our socialist and democratic ideology....
>
> Rather, it is a matter of clarifying the function of the party at the time of the *sursaut national*, of determining its role in our

123

program of economic and financial recovery, and of deciding
how it can best contribute to the preservation and consolidation
of our democratic system, so as to make it irreversible.... The
politics of renewal must permeate the party if it is to acquire a
vigorous national impetus.[1]

The renewal of the party did not imply, however, a total
change in its structures and orientation, neither did it involve
forcing the militants into accepting policies and new leaders
imposed from on high. What it called for was an effective
combination of discipline, unity, and democracy. Diouf
argued:

> Our future victories can only be guaranteed through internal
> democracy.... Democracy implies the fight against certain
> practices such as *parachutage*, corruption, opportunism,
> favoritism.... We must also strengthen our discipline ... to impose
> the slogans and the doctrine of the party.... Discipline and
> democracy are the key words....
> True democracy within the party consists of neither
> exclusion nor discrimination, but rather of opening it to all its
> militants.
> I specify that *parachutage* is ... the imposition from above of
> leaders on the rank and file.[2]

The practice of democracy within the PS was not to eclipse,
however, the strong leadership of Diouf. As secretary general of
the PS, Diouf was to be the source and director of all major
ideological pronouncements and practical policies.[3] If there
was to be democracy, there was to be also the hegemonic presence
of President Diouf. Such hegemony was further reinforced in
April of 1983 when the position of prime minister was abolished
to give way to a presidential system.[4] Diouf justified the
establishment of a strong presidentialism in terms of
simplifying and rationalizing the functioning of the
government:

> The government, which is in charge of conducting the policy of
> renewal at this particularly difficult time, must be able to
> accomplish its mission with more efficiency, rapidity, and
> simplicity. The government must therefore act under the direct
> authority of the head of state.
> We must now proceed with the institutional changes that will
> permit the head of state to directly lead, animate, and control the
> administration. It is for this reason which responds

only to the necessities related to the efficient, harmonious, and rapid functioning of the state, that I am submitting to the national assembly a constitutional revision calling for the elimination of the post of prime minister. I must emphasize, however, that by taking this decision, I intend to conform only to the national interest and to the wish expressed by the Senegalese people for engaging directly the responsibility of the head of state in the making of public policy.[5]

Having expanded his power, Diouf could now implement his own agenda, unrestrained by constitutional limitations and internal political challenges. Diouf's presidentialism strengthened not only his control of the government, it also reinforced his leadership of and established his uncontested political supremacy over the Parti socialiste to steer it in the direction that he saw fit. It is in this context that his appeals for national unity must be understood.

These appeals expressed the necessity for a broad consensus, but it was a consensus that had to be based on the existing policies and programs of the PS. They never implied the possibility of a government departing from the fundamental doctrines and options of the PS.

The national consensus ... is a national process that must permit different parties, groupings, and individuals to act together to confront the problems that we are all confronting—whether we are in the opposition or in the ruling party. Such a consensus is not directed against anyone in particular, nor against the opposition, and least of all against the PS.... National consensus is neither cordial entente, nor the 'the peace of the brave'; it is rather the mutual promise of conscious and responsible partners who refuse to succumb to the vicissitudes that nature and circumstance have imposed on us. Consensus thus implies:

   a.   That all political formations accept the rules of the democratic game, while displaying loyalty towards the republican institutions, and respecting the democratic principles that they will help preserve and strengthen.
   b.   That all political formations defend and come to an agreement to serve the national interest.
   c.   That the opposition be constructive instead of being destructive and preoccupied with power.
   d.   That the ruling party demonstrate ... openness and tolerance that recognize that the opposition should also have its own sphere of activity, and that it too should be involved in the search for solutions to our national problems.[6]

This generous impulse toward the opposition was negated, however, by Diouf's own determined will to preserve and expand the hold of the PS on the reigns of government. According to him the politics of the *sursaut national* was based on

> the conviction that political pluralism is the democratic system best adapted to our people, and that all cadres—irrespective of their politics, ethnicity, religion, and ideology—participate in the development of the nation. However, this does not in the least imply that the party should be deprived of its governmental authority. After all, the government received a mandate to apply faithfully and loyally the policy and program of the Socialist party. The government is indissolubly linked to the PS to which it owes everything.[7]

Diouf's appeals for a national consensus were therefore directed more at independent and competent individuals than at the parties of the opposition. It is true, however, that upon assuming the presidency, Diouf made a concerted effort at conciliation. Not only did he legalize unlimited pluralism, but he also convened a national congress on education to resolve the explosive crisis in the universities and schools. The militant Syndicat unique et démocratique des enseignants (SUDES), which had called in 1980 for a general strike of teachers and professors to demand increases in salaries and a major reform of the educational system, and which consequently endured the repressive measures of Senghor's regime, participated actively in the national congress.[8]   Diouf's appeal for a national consensus was not merely a symbolic gesture devoid of substance, it sought to reestablish peace and harmony in a society that had increasingly been polarized and divided in the last years of Senghor's presidency.

It is also true that certain sectors of the opposition advanced the idea of a "Senegalese historical compromise" entailing a government of "national unity" and regrouping a "maximum of political families" under the leadership of President Diouf.[9] Mar Fall may thus have been correct when he argued that Senegalese politics had entered a collaborative era in the middle of 1983.[10]   As we have seen, however, Diouf's insistence on imposing on the opposition the total supremacy of the PS, and his rejection of any significant modifications in the policies and programs of his government, seriously eroded the prospects of a Senegalese historical compromise.

In fact the president's appeals for a national consensus represented more an effort to integrate into the PS a new generation of young technocrats and organic intellectuals, than a meaningful attempt to draw the opposition into the government. These appeals could not satisfy the opposition since they inevitably implied its total subordination to the policies and program of the Parti socialiste. While the PS claimed that these policies embodied the essence of a democratic socialism, they bore the unmistakable imprint of the major international organs of financial capitalism on which Senegal depended for its economic survival.

Such dependence forced the Dioufist regime to embark on a major program of austerity and "destatization." In the eyes of the regime these two objectives did not contradict its democratic socialist orientation. The process of privatization of the economy was seen not as an obstacle to this orientation, but as its necessary complement. In his *Rapport Introductif* to the national council of the PS, President Diouf insisted on the correspondence between democratic socialism and a strong private sector:

> For us, the dynamism and competitiveness of the private sector constitute a means of realizing our socialist and democratic objective. Development, which is a general process, cannot be only the business of the state. Development, in our specific situation, occurs when it involves the efforts of everyone. This is the principle of economic democracy, which is an indispensable condition of democratic socialism, since all the social forces are involved in production, in the distribution of revenues, and in the promotion of employment, liberties, and leisure.[11]

The decline of state interventionism in the economy, however, stemmed more from the orthodox monetary demands of international organs of financial capitalism such as the IMF and the World Bank, than from the Parti socialiste's belief in the alleged compatibility between socialism and privatization. As Cheikh Hamidou Kane, the minister for planning and cooperation, acknowledged, Senegal's economic options were constrained and they had to be adjusted "to take into account the new orientation being outlined by international lending institutions that demand a clear and precise definition of economic policies before extending their support to any program of investments."[12] This implied the implementation of austerity measures to bring state expenditures into line with revenues; such measures have inevitably led to profound limitations on the growth of the money supply and to drastic reductions in public and social spendings.[13] Privatization and austerity reflect, first and foremost, the contradiction between the declining room for maneuver available to Senegal's policy makers and their increasing dependence on external institutions for financing their nation's development.

This declining room for maneuver has generated a political and social malaise as the reduction in local purchasing power and welfare expenditures has led to greater unemployment and to a lower standard of living for the masses. In a poor country like Senegal where the majority of the population barely reaches a minimum level of subsistence, the decision to impose a program of strict economic austerity can only have negative and adverse political consequences. In addition, however the government may have wanted to justify privatization and austerity, they have both contradicted its socialist doctrine and its long-term goals of economic and political self-reliance.

It is true that, short of a socialist revolution bent on escaping the gravitational pull of the world industrial civilization, very few realistic alternatives are left to Senegalese policymakers. They may aim at minimizing the cost of dependence by developing more self-reliant agricultural and industrial policies based on domestic production, resources, and consumption. Such a "basic needs" strategy, however, would require so many structural reforms at both the internal and international levels that it also would inevitably necessitate a revolution. As Richard Sandbrook argues:

> In the context of an assault on poverty, the line between structural reform and revolution is hazy indeed. The scope of change necessitated by a basic-needs strategy is vast. There needs to be simultaneous action in the economic sphere (to change the pattern of national growth and the use of productive resources, and perhaps the international economic order), in social structure (as a result of changes in the distribution of assets, income and public services), and, if the goal of popular participation is taken seriously, in the sphere of political institutions as well.... [It] is most unlikely that change of this scope and abruptness could occur without the prod or threat of violent upheaval.[14]

It is in this context of limited options short of a truly revolutionary alternative that the opposition's critiques and solutions must be understood. While the critiques were coherent, severe, and probably correct, the solutions, when they existed at all, were never programmatic nor explicit. Pathé Diagne observes that

> political formations have not yet ... deemed it necessary to mobilize their intellectual, technical, and scientific cadres.... They merely issue vague projects and declarations of principles, while jealously concealing ... whatever short- or long-term program they may have developed.[15]

The opposition's relative failure to formulate a coherent programmatic alternative to the PS has been compounded by its numerous attempts to unite in a common front different parties of diverse and contradicting ideological currents. As we shall see, such attempts have inevitably hampered the development of clear policies since differences had to be glossed over for the sake of unity. What was proposed for the resolution of the social and economic crisis was consequently sketchy and incidental, amounting to vague declarations of intention to eradicate poverty, unemployment, and corruption. How these objectives were to be realized remained a question without an explicit answer.

As individual entities, the parties of the opposition offered clearer and more ambitious programs, even if such programs never constituted fully developed alternatives to the ruling policies of the PS. Let us briefly examine the programs of the major parties of the opposition.

The Parti Démocratique Sénégalais (PDS)

The doctrine and policies of the PDS bear the strong influence of its founder and leader Abdoulaye Wade who advocates an African form of *socialisme-travailliste.* For Wade, it is based on three fundamental elements:

> A theory of production, a theory of distribution, a theory of development....
> Because our countries are rich in manpower and poor in capital, it is wiser to adopt labor-intensive forms of production....

The privileged position thus accorded to Senegalese labor and human resources insures also a fairer distribution of social benefits since salaries distributed to workers will tend to increase to the detriment of profits accruing to capitalists....

The implications of such a vision are very important ... agriculture ought to be the basis of our development since it corresponds to the activities of more than 90 percent of the population....

To make agriculture the basis of our development is to put the Senegalese himself in charge of development instead of always relying on foreign aid....

We believe that work is the source of freedom and thus our doctrine is permeated by a mystique of work similar to that of the Murids. This reference to mysticism is not in the least surprising since many types of European socialism have been inspired by christian mysticism.[16]

Wade's *socialisme-travailliste*, however, was quite different from its European counterpart. Whereas the latter found its articulation in its association with the trade union movement, the former was based on the Murid brotherhoods' understanding of work as the means of becoming a follower and disciple of God. Work, in Wade's *socialisme-travailliste*, is sanctified by and embedded in the Murid's Islamic ethic. Islam, in this view, can do for Senegalese development what Protestantism did for European capitalism.[17] In addition to this religious inspiration, the *pensée négro-Africaine* imparts to Wade's *socialisme-travailliste* the unique notion that freedom stems from the process of working and creating.

In its *Programme fondamental du socialisme-travailliste*, adopted in 1976, the PDS established the specificity of its doctrine by contrasting it to what it considered the two dominant forms of European socialism: Marxism-Leninism and Christian socialism. According to the PDS, both Marxism-Leninism and Christian socialism are deficient because the first rejects freedom during the period of the dictatorship of the proletariat to accept it only in the last phase of history—communism, and because the second makes it an absolute preceding the existence of society itself. In opposition to these two views, the PDS asserted that

the originality of Negro African thought consists in accepting freedom during [the period of the dictatorship of the proletariat] and in considering it linked to socialism through the labor process. This vision rests on an analysis of the relationship existing between the community and the individual.

The African mind cannot conceive of the individual as an alien entity separate from the community—both form a single structure. It understands in the same way *socialism*, the aspiration of the community, and *freedom*, the aspiration of the individual. But socialism and freedom are ... an ideal state that we seek to attain through *work* ... which is the foundation of progress.

It follows that the social project of the PDS is based on three fundamental and interdependent values: *socialism, freedom, and work*.[18]

The primacy that the PDS gives to work implies the adoption of a strategy based on peasant labor and thus on agriculture. Such a strategy of "non-industrial growth" envisages the diversification of agricultural production, which becomes the central motor of a self-reliant alternative of economic development. It is an alternative that seeks to eliminate the most severe patterns of Senegalese dependence implanted by the incompetence of Diouf's regime. According to Wade, the policies of the Parti socialiste have led to the complete submission of Senegal to foreign financial powers; and these policies have exacerbated the economic crisis and failed to generate a coherent process of growth. As Wade explained in his opening speech to the congress of the PDS in 1982:

[The situation that Senegal faces] ... is characterized by an economic, financial, and social crisis of a severity and breadth never known before....

The simple and only truth ... is that our country, our dear Senegal, is quite simply mortaged for the next twelve years....

The PS government has, in effect, concluded with Senegal's creditors ... a general agreement according to which Senegal cannot engage in any financial activity for the next twelve years ... without the explicit backing of these creditors.[19]

To prevent the further deterioration of the economy, the PDS has proposed a *Plan de redressement* that seeks to transform the material foundations of Senegal in the direction of a self-centered agricultural mode of development. This mode of development, the PDS argues, would break away from the existing neocolonial system implanted by the governing Parti socialiste. As Wade continued:

I believe that this system, which is nothing but the continuation of colonialism, is bad and has to be changed.

Our party's program of recovery rests on this conviction, and on the need for a *total restructuring of the national economy*....The IMF speaks only of structural adjustments and grants loans to that end when, in reality, the problem of Senegal is the complete restructuring of the economy through a new redistribution of sectorial activities, and through reorganization and regulation. The priority we give to agriculture would by itself transform existing economic structures, and, in the secondary sector, the essential role would be played by export industries using very little capital....

The priority accorded to agriculture, if effectively implemented ... would radically change the structures of the economy, and turn upside down the Western model of development....[20]

The PDS program, except for its commitment to invest 15 billion francs CFA for three consecutive years in the agricultural sector in the form of a free distribution of seeds and fertilizers, does not differ markedly from those embodied in the different five-year plans of the PS, which have all miserably failed. In fact, as Wade has himself acknowledged, a PDS government would have to deal with the IMF and the World Bank in order to finance investments and repay the Senegalese debt. The fundamental difference would be that such a PDS government would be led by more competent individuals who would be able to implement the restructuring of the economy because they would be unencumbered by the weight of decades of *la politique politicienne*.[21] This implies that, the failure of the PS is not necessarily the failure of its ideological vision, but the failure of the men who have tried to implement it. According to Wade, these men, and in particular Abdou Diouf, have been incapable of establishing a credible and popular government without which no solution to the crisis is possible. As he argued in an interview in *Takusaan*:

Abdou Diouf will never resolve the crisis because he does not seem to know the source of the problem.... The government is at the stage of what economists call an uncoordinated oligopoly.... An orchestra, even when its individual members are excellent musicians, needs a conductor who imparts rhythm and harmony. If each musician, however talented, improvises, then it is cacophony.... We must thus cease to deceive ourselves: no one believes in the stability of the present regime.[22]

The emphasis on personal incompetence indicates that the programmatic differences between the PDS and the PS are not so fundamental as to preclude the possibility of a government of national unity. In fact, when President Diouf called for the establishment of a national consensus in July 1983, the PDS was the only party of the opposition to respond positively. Not only did it end its five-month-old parliamentary boycott, which had symbolized its rejection of the results of the 1983 elections, but its secretary general, Abdoulaye Wade, also agreed to meet Diouf to discuss the idea of the national consensus.

That Wade now describes his acceptance of the meeting as a political mistake and rejects any program of national unity with the current PS regime is more a reflection of his utter contempt for Diouf's leadership capacities than of his opposition to such a program of national unity.[23] In Wade's view, national unity is indeed more necessary than ever, given the present economic, social, and political conjuncture, but it requires certain basic and minimal conditions which Diouf and his administration preclude. In his interview in *Takusaan*, he explained that

> a large consensus around a national program.... is clearly impossible as long as the PS and Abdou Diouf continue to assert that which only they themselves believe: that they won the elections and that such a victory confers on them special rights.
>
> At least three conditions are required for a man or a party to save this country....
>
> First, power must not be a simple assertion of authority. Power must be supported by a real majority, or at least a large consensus. Since no party in Senegal has such a majority it is therefore necessary to establish a consensus among the different political formations.
>
> Then, the new government must be capable of obtaining without delay the capital necessary for fueling the economic recovery. Only a credible and popular government will obtain such foreign assistance....
>
> Finally, ... the government must be able to effect those structural transformations without which nothing of lasting value will be possible.[24]

What Wade calls for, however, is quite compatible with the programs and policies of the IMF and the World Bank which the current PS administration is implementing. Indeed, Wade's project rests on the promotion of agriculture as the primary and fundamental motor of development and on a process of export-oriented industrialization requiring little capital and technology. Such a project is congruent with the emerging new international specialization of labor that confines Third World nations to the production of cheap, labor-intensive manufacturing goods to be exported to the core capitalist countries, which would in turn monopolize the production of technologically advanced and capital-intensive goods. Moreover, this hierarchical division of nations would be further accentuated by the priority given to agricultural production since this involves neglecting the development of an industrial sector grounded in domestic production and needs. Accordingly, Wade's strategy of economic growth might well lead to the total "peripheralization" of Senegal as a non-industrialized zone condemned to agricultural backwardness. As Pathé Diagne remarks:

> The strategy of "agriculture [as the] basis of industry" or "non-industrial development" has succeeded nowhere. It is merely one of the recipes of the developed countries and the World Bank to "specialize" the Third World and maintain the exploitative international division.... The long-term strategy of the PDS is similar to that which the UPS/PS has implemented for the last twenty-five years without ever realizing its objectives.
>
> The PDS, like the PS and the IMF, is counting on ... the hazards of a capricious Sahelian agriculture to bring about the recovery. The injection of 45 billion francs into the peanut sector may contribute only to further plunge the state into debt and increase the deficits in the balance of payments.... The economic programs of the PS and PDS surrender to "the prohibition of domestic industrialization" dictated by the advanced countries and the IMF.... These programs cannot promote true structural transformations, or even the creation of effective and productive primary and secondary sectors. In fact, the programs of the PS and PDS are prisoners of the policies developed by the IMF and the industrialized powers....[25]

It is precisely this issue of dissociation from the world capitalist economy and its main financial organs that differentiates the PS and PDS from the other Senegalese political parties. These parties have generally advocated some form of dissociation, whether it be partial, total, or temporary. They tend to be grouped into four main political families and concepts; let us briefly analyze these four concepts and the strategies that they entail.

The *Révolution Nationale Démocratique et Populaire*

The concept of the *révolution nationale démocratique et populaire* (RNDP) stems from the tradition of Chinese and Vietnamese Marxism. It is founded on the belief that the backwardness of the productive forces in Third World countries precludes the immediate ushering in of a pure proletarian society. Accordingly, a period of transition towards such a society is required, and this in turn creates the conditions for certain strategic alliances and objectives that form the basis of the RNDP.

In spite of ideological and tactical differences, the Mouvement démocratique populaire (MDP) of Mamadou Dia, the AND/JEF Mouvement révolutionaire pour la démocratie nouvelle (AND-JEF/MRDN) of Landing Savane, and the Union pour la démocratie populaire (UDP) of Racine Guisse, have subscribed to the RNDP program. As defined by AND-JEF/MRDN, the RNDP is a necessary revolutionary process in the struggle against the neocolonial PS regime:

> *The neocolonial system retards the development of the productive forces, lowers the standard of living of the working population, makes insecurity a normal condition, maintains the people who are directly subjected to it ignorant and without rights, and causes, in turn, discontent and revolt.*
>
> Thus, the *suppression of the evil from which our masses suffer necessarily depends on the overthrow of the neocolonial system.* This is why the *révolution nationale démocratique et populaire* (RNDP) for the *creation of a new and democratic society* must become the program of struggle of the Senegalese people. This revolution is *anti-imperialistic, anti-hegemonic, and anti-feudal.* Its major targets are French imperialism, the political-bureaucratic bourgeoisie, the *comprador* bourgeoisie, and semifeudal exploiters.
>
> The RNDP activates all the anti-imperialist forces. It unites under the leadership of the proletariat and the peasantry, the petite bourgeoisie and the patriotic faction of the national bourgeoisie.
>
> The RNDP seeks   both to eliminate the imperialist domination of our country and end feudal oppression.[26]

The RNDP is a revolution that must be first and foremost national, that is, it must eliminate all manifestations of imperialism and neocolonialism. Such a goal presupposes that the revolution be democratic and, therefore, that it emancipates the peasantry and the working class from the repressive obscurantism of semifeudal agricultural practices and urban bureaucratic capitalism. Finally, the revolution must not be the product of a sole vanguard and elitist party, it must be popular and as such it must be grounded in the hegemony of the proletariat and peasant classes.[27]

The RNDP is a stage in the revolutionary process leading to socialism. This stage or *l'état de démocratie nouvelle* will be characterized by an alliance of all "patriotic and progressive" classes under the leadership of the peasantry and proletariat. The alliance will revolutionize the social system as a whole and it will seek the liquidation of the ruling *comprador* and bureaucratic bourgeoisies, as well as all semifeudal exploiters. The government will constitute a united revolutionary front of all anti-imperialist forces. The front would therefore comprise the progressive wings of the national bourgeoisie and petite bourgeoisie, but it would come under the undisputed leadership of the proletariat and peasantry. In this sense, the front seeks to establish the hegemony of the working classes.

As explained by AND–JEF/MRDN, the fundamental objective of the RNDP is the establishment of a new and popular state embodied in the formation of *l'état de démocratie nouvelle* whose task is:

> To establish people's power
> To develop an independent and planned economy under the
>   control of the state
> To effect agrarian reforms on the basis of the principle: *the land
>   shall belong to those who labor on it*
> To insure the well-being of the people
> To promote a national, popular, and scientific culture
> To safeguard national independence and promote the
>   adequate defense of the homeland from annexationist and
>   aggressive threats from wherever they may originate.
>
> *The elimination of the neocolonial system cannot be
> accomplished rapidly.* The indispensable transformation of the
> balance of power in favor of the people ... can only be carried out
> *progressively*, during the course of a long process that will know
> successes and failures until final victory.
>   The people's triumph will depend on *counting above all on
> one's own strength,* and on following carefully an autonomous
> and independent policy from all foreign parties or country.[28]

These objectives, however noble, constitute a program that

does not go beyond general themes and revolutionary slogans. Although it represents a coherent and powerful critique of the government, the RNDP remains a highly theoretical and abstract statement of intentions that clearly lacks specificity.[29] While it seeks to establish the hegemony of the proletariat and the peasantry, it fails to explain how this hegemony can crystallize as a living practice. It is difficult to imagine the realization of such hegemony since the national bourgeoisie, however progressive it may be, is to participate in the making of the *état de démocratie nouvelle*. Indeed, how and why would the bourgeoisie accept its subordination to the working classes in this *état*? On this fundamental issue, the RNDP program is at best elusive and vague.

The RNDP, however, represents a clear indictment of the ruling PS regime. This regime is defined as neocolonial and subordinate to the organs of international capitalism. Instead of consolidating the gains of political independence, it has accentuated the ties of dependence; instead of creating a popular government, it has degenerated into a "pseudoliberal democracy," and, instead of working for the collective good, it has promoted the selfish corporate interests of a parasitic bureaucratic bourgeoisie. The indictment of both the Senghor and Diouf governments is the most severe. In the words of Landing Savane—the secretary general of AND–JEF/MRDN—independence has brought very little to the Senegalese people.

> [Independence] has materialized in the *emergence and consolidation of a bureaucratic bourgeoisie,* which has confiscated power and exercized it for the benefit of its imperialist masters within the framework of *anti-national, anti-democratic, and anti-popular policies....*
> The current *diktat* of the IMF over the economic and financial policies of the government, the persistent monopolization by foreign capital (especially French) of the economic activity of our country, and the presence since 'independence' of French interventionist troops on our national soil are all significant indications of such antinational orientation.... Surrounded on all sides by the catastrophic consequences of its economic policy, the government was forced to appeal to the IMF to avoid total bankruptcy.... Today, the plan of recovery will fuel a galloping inflation ... that will further aggravate the problems confronting the Senegalese masses ... and the government will continue to implement its current

antipopular policies in the coming years.[30]

These harsh denunciations of goverment policies, however justified they may be, have not produced a coherent programmatic alternative. The RNDP program suffers from a form of escapism that clouds serious and explicit thinking about the means of achieving the promised socialist society. Insofar as the RNDP envisaged the future in programmatic terms, the vision remained almost exclusively political. It promised the establishment of *l'état de démocratie nouvelle* without specifying how this state could come into being and how it would assure the hegemony of the peasant and proletarian forces. It promised a total dissociation from imperialism and capitalism without clearly explaining the difficult mechanisms of such a dissociation. Indeed, the RNDP's statements on economic policy are sketchy and elliptical, amounting to vague and general proposals for the transformation of agriculture, the nationalization of major industries, and the installation of state planning. Because of its perfunctory attention to the radical transformation of the existing neocolonial economy, the RNDP represents a programmatic and intellectual vacuum that has yet to constitute a viable alternative to current policies and strategies.

Such a vacuum is also evident in the socialist visions entailed in the remaining three concepts to which we now turn our attention.

The *République Démocratique Sénégalaise*

The concept of the *république démocratique sénégalaise* (RDS) constitutes the Parti africain de l'indépendance's (PAI) program of transition to socialism. It is based on the conviction that the immediate objective of any revolution is the implantation of a real and effective independence from neocolonial forces. Such an objective requires the creation of an alliance of all progressive and patriotic classes. As the PAI states in its program:

> The proletariat, the peasantry, the urban petite bourgeoisie (commercial or industrial), and the patriotic elements belonging to the other strata of the population are enslaved and exploited in differing degrees by foreign imperialism.

> Thus, fundamentally, they have an interest in national liberation—that is to say, in real independence, and in the elimination of the colonial and neocolonial imperialist system.[31]

It is this rupture with imperialism that creates the conditions for the establishment of the RDS. The RDS would therefore be based on a real independence, which would in turn facilitate the process of social, economic, and cultural development. Such development would rest on the expansion of democratic rights and on the nationalization of the major organs of production and exchange. This would not usher in socialism, but it would guarantee a planned industrialization turned toward the satisfaction of domestic needs through the use and transformation of domestic resources and materials. The RDS represents, therefore, a minimal program of social change that would generate the material conditions for the transition to socialism.

That the RDS embodies a minimal program does not imply that its realization would be simple. In fact, the RDS is possible at all only because the world system is no longer dominated by reactionary forces. The socialist revolutions, as well as the success of the movements of national liberation, have contributed to the weakening of imperialism and, thereby, to the development of progressive political and economic alternatives. Such revolutionary achievements, according to the PAI, have created a favorable terrain for the immediate building of a Senegalese democratic republic (the RDS).[32]

The PAI, even with inscribing the RDS on its immediate political agenda, has failed to explain how such a RDS would come into being. While it is true that the PAI favors a *Front uni sénégalais* to conquer political power and establish the basis of the RDS, it has provided little programmatic information on the means and methods conducive to both the Front uni sénégalais and the RDS. As a Marxist organization, the PAI desires the transformation of society in a socialist direction, but these desires have not gone beyond the level of aspirations and promises. The absence of specific and meaningful policies is reflected in comments by Majhemout Diop (the leader of PAI) on the composition and nature of the RDS: "The RDS requires an alliance of patriotic anti-imperialist classes that excludes the agents of neocolonialism.... In due time, the Senegalese people will find the best way to establish the RDS."[33]

The vagueness of the RDS program is further exacerbated by the emphasis that it places on the necessity of pan-Africanism. In the eyes of the PAI, Senegal's development and the RDS itself will always be constrained by the constrictions of micronationalism. Diop explains:

> We have never believed, and we do not believe in micronationalism....
> In the current conjuncture, even with a good government, Senegal could barely improve its economy, and no more.
> Pan-Africanism, and even better, pan-Negroism, are historical necessities, and they shall remain so forever.[34]

Socialism and economic growth in Senegal itself depend on the political and material unity of the African continent. However justified and correct this view may be, it fails to elucidate the processes and means required for its very crystallization. The RDS and the pan-Africanism that it implies represent nothing more than noble aspirations and promises; they have yet to become operative plans and policies.

Similar limitations and failures characterize the concepts of *révolution démocratique nationale and révolution nationale démocratique*, the respective programs of the Ligue démocratique/Mouvement pour le parti du travail (LD/MPT) and the Parti de l'indépendance et du travail-Sénégal (PIT-S). That these two concepts, in spite of certain ideological and political differences, are broadly congruent with the RDS should come as no surprise since both the LD/MPT and the PIT-S share the Marxist orientation of PAI, from which they splintered.[35]

The *Révolution Démocratique Nationale*

The *révolution démocratique nationale* (RDN) constitutes the program of transition to socialism adopted by the Ligue démocratique/ Mouvement pour le parti du travail (LD/MPT). It is based on the idea that the placing of Senegal on the periphery of the world capitalist system has blocked the development of the productive forces and so prevented the flowering of the objective conditions conducive to the immediate bringing in of socialism. A period of transition during which certain class alliances are established and certain social compromises are tolerated is therefore required; this period of transition embodies the RDN.

The RDN, however, presupposes the "liquidation" of the existing neocolonial regime and the subsequent installation of proletarian hegemony under the vanguard leadership of the LD/MPT. The LD/MPT explains that

> the *révolution démocratique nationale* ... will make possible both the accumulation of capital and the democratic reforms that are necessary for establishing the objective and subjective bases of socialism. The necessity of this stage, however, does not in any way eliminate the role of the proletariat in its struggle against the bourgeoisie, nor does it suppress the need for the proletariat's own party and ideology. The RDN requires only that the proletarian party applies and develops creatively a policy of alliances that takes into consideration the current conditions of our society, particularly the unique class structure, the existing distribution of power between progressive and reactionary forces, and the original means and specific stages of the revolutionary process in progress.[36]

The RDN is based on an alliance of classes headed by the proletariat and led by a vanguard proletarian party whose task is to organize and impose the hegemony of a Senegalese form of Marxism-Leninism. The question this inevitably raises is what are the forces of reaction that are to be excluded from, and what are the forces of progress that are to be included in, this alliance of classes. According to the LD/MPT, Senegalese society is divided into five main classes, some of which are in turn divided into conflicting factions and strata.

The bourgeoisie is comprised of three factions. The first is foreign; it dominates the major economic sectors of Senegal, and it is a source of constant exploitation of labor. This foreign bourgeoisie is allied to the bureaucratic and *comprador* bourgeoisie, which controls the state as a neocolonial appendage of imperialism. Both the foreign and bureaucratic-*comprador* bourgeoisies are parasitic classes that cannot be integrated into the progressive alliance inherent in the RDN. In fact, the RDN is impossible without their political annihilation. In contrast, the third, national bourgeoisie, in spite of its conservative tendencies, represents an objective (if only temporary) ally of the proletariat.[37]

The feudal aristocracy is similarly divided into a reactionary and potentially patriotic faction. Whereas the reactionary wing has a profoundly conservative influence on the peasantry and tends to support the political and economic

objectives of the foreign and bureaucratic-*comprador*
bourgeoisies, the patriotic wing identifies with the more
progressive aspirations of the national bourgeoisie. These
circumstances create the possibility of an integration of this
patriotic wing of the feudal aristocracy into the bloc of classes
comprising the RDN.[38]

The third major class is the petite bourgeoisie, which
constitutes a heterogeneous class whose consciousness, however
vague it may be, can be radicalized under the influence of a
proletarian party. To this extent, it embodies a potential ally of
the working class. Moreover, it is a class from which may
spring many radical intellectuals capable of shaping the
ideological contours of the RDN.[39]

The fourth, and most important, class is the proletariat,
which in spite of being young, weak, and small, represents the
historical class; this is the class that will wage the revolutionary
struggle for a communist society under the necessary
organizational and political leadership of a vanguard
proletarian party. As the official program of the LD/MPT
contends:

> Today, [the proletariat] is capable of assuming its historical role,
> provided that it has at its disposal the necessary ideology and
> party—Marxism-Leninism and the Communist party
> respectively. The only requirement that the specificity of our
> national situation demands is a creative policy of alliances.... The
> Senegalese working class has the potential to achieve such an
> objective.[40]

To become the hegemonic class of the RDN, the proletariat must
win the allegiance and loyalty of the largest Senegalese class,
the peasantry.

In contrast to the conjunctural and transitional character of
the alliance with the national bourgeoisie, petite bourgeoisie,
and the patriotic wing of the feudal aristocracy, the alliance
between proletariat and peasantry is strategic and, indeed, it is
the means of guaranteeing the establishment of socialism. As
the LD/MPT states in its program:

> As the overwhelming majority of our people and the most
> oppressed class, [the peasantry] ... constitutes the principal force
> ... on which the success or failure of the *révolution démocratique
> nationale* depends. The peasantry can either lead or follow the
> bourgeoisie. In its struggle against the bour-

geoisie—waged at all stages of the revolutionary process—the
Senegalese proletariat must win over the peasantry.... Properly
guided by the Communist party, the peasantry ... will be able to
participate fully in the construction of socialism. This is why the
LD/MPT does not see the alliance between the working class and
the peasantry as temporary, but rather as strategic.[41]

The peasant-proletarian alliance is therefore the historical
bloc that will give to the RDN its socialist orientation. Without
it, the "democratic dictatorship" of the proletariat and the
peasantry entailed by the RDN would fail to materialize. Even
though this "democratic dictatorship" constitutes a
revolutionary state, it will preserve "pluralism, the right of
association, and religious freedoms." As explained by the
LD/MPT its main political organs will consist of

the popular assembly, the assembly in which the deputy workers,
peasants, soldiers, and revolutionary intellectuals will be
hegemonic. The functioning and organization of state power will
be based on democratic centralism, which will allow the people to
express their will and defeat the enemies of the revolution. Each
administrative division will be assigned a popular assembly....
The hypocrisy of bourgeois parliamentary democracy will thus
be abolished, and with it bureaucratic inefficiency.[42]

In this sense, the "democratic dictatorship" of the RDN is a
stage in the process leading to the creation of a pure proletarian
dictatorship. The LD/MPT, however, fails to explain the method
of bringing about this "democratic dictatorship": Will the
"democratic dictatorship" originate from the universal
suffrage of liberal bourgeois tradition, or will it require a
revolutionary break from such tradition? It is true that the RDN
is more explicit than the RNDP on the role of the revolutionary
party in the building of the new society. Indeed, while the RNDP
tends to emphasize *l'initiative créatrice* of the working classes
and thus minimizes the directing role of the party in the
revolutionary process, the RDN establishes unambiguously the
primary and determining place of a vanguard Communist
party in the organization, mobilization, and radicalization of
the proletariat and the peasantry.

The RDN, however, like the RNDP, suffers from serious
programmatic deficiencies. Its major objectives are to achieve

food self-sufficiency and full employment and to establish effectively the citizens' rights to housing, education, health, and leisure. To fulfill these objectives, the RDN proposes a twofold strategy that would, on the one hand, radically transform the agricultural sector and, on the other, increase the role of the state in the economy. A massive redistribution of land according to the principle of "the land to those who till it" would be effected in conjunction with the infrastructural development of the rural sector and the nationalization of all the commanding heights of the economy. This in turn, would require "the establishment of both scientific management and rigorous planning of national resources through a comprehensive economic plan."[43]

How to obtain the financial resources for such a radical transformation of Senegalese society is an issue that remains unanswered. One must also wonder—even if these resources were available—what would be the political means used to confront the inevitable resistance of both the ruling class and its powerful foreign allies. Confronted with such drastic problems the LD/MPT can only quote Lenin: "The difficulties are immense, but the revolution is nothing but a triumph over immense difficulties!"[44] It is true that, while acknowledging such limitations, the LD/MPT is in the process of elaborating a *programme de la transition* that should elucidate the economic project of its socialist vision, but, for the moment only vague generalizations exist.[45] This, however, does not suffice to make a coherent revolutionary economic program. Similar limitations characterize the concept of *révolution nationale démocratique* adopted by the Parti de l'indépendance et du travail—Sénégal (PIT-S).

The *Révolution Nationale Démocratique*

The *révolution nationale démocratique* (RND) gives primacy to the national and anti-imperialist struggle over and above the immediate quest for proletarian and peasant hegemony. This is what distinguishes it from the RDN, with which it is otherwise almost identical. The analysis will therefore be brief and confined to a more detailed examination of this distinction.

Whereas the RDN is based on the necessity of establishing the immediate hegemony of the working classes prior to the crystallization of socialism, the RND seems to favor a more nationalist course insofar as it would promote the economic development of the national bourgeoisie.   In its program of action, the PIT-S declares:

> Senegalese businessmen must finally occupy the place that is theirs in the economic structure of the country.... *The real solution being that the national bourgeoisie gain access to profitable sectors by ending the traditional anachronism and the economic discriminations favoring the French monopolies and the Lebanese bourgeoisie.* A wide range of profitable activities must be reserved exclusively for Senegalese businessmen.[46]

Such a policy would not necessarily imply the acceptance of a form of state capitalism, but it would signify that, for a transitional period, the formation of an anti-imperialist and nationalist bloc would have priority over the struggle for socialism.   It is difficult, however, to understand how the economic promotion of the national bourgeoisie can be reconciled with the PIT-S's contention that "capitalism, for the overwhelming majority of the populations living in the areas of the movements of national liberation,... is incapable of solving the problems of independence, of insuring rapid economic and social progress, and of overcoming the specific contradictions of underdevelopment...."[47]   An apparent contradiction exists between the active material contribution of the national bourgeoisie to the building of the RND and the recognition that capitalist growth in a peripheral country like Senegal can only generate the development of underdevelopment.   This is a contradiction that the PIT-S has yet to resolve satisfactorily. True enough, an alliance that is more than just conjunctural with the national bourgeoisie would enhance the stability and durability of a postrevolutionary regime, but it might, in the process, block the ascendancy of socialist forces and policies.

The RND, as envisioned by the PIT-S, is full of ambiguity. Although it is based on the conviction that capitalism cannot generate the social and economic development of Senegal, it nonetheless seeks an alliance with the national bourgeoisie in an anti-imperialist and anticapitalist bloc.   Why and how the national bourgeoisie would accept its demise as a potential ruling class is an issue on which the RND remains vague and elliptical.

Similarly, instead of offering a clear and specific alternative to current governmental policies, the RND fails—except for a few broad and general remarks on the necessity of increasing the role of the state and of nationalizing key industries—to articulate a viable economic plan commensurate with its revolutionary ambitions and socialist vision. Thus, while the RND as well as the RDS, RDN, and RNDP represent a severe and cogent critical indictment of current governmental policies, they all suffer from a programmatic escapism embodied in the relative absence of specific plans and policies for a post-PS revolutionary regime. Pathé Diagne sums up the situation:

> Both the government and the opposition are deadlocked in an impasse that requires, whether we like it or not, a coherent program of precise solutions, and a large popular consensus.... The political debate on the Senegalese economic and financial crisis is of interest only from this perspective. For the moment, the debate stammers.[48]

In an attempt to move away from such an impasse, the parties of the opposition have attempted on numerous occasions to form united fronts that would offer a serious and majority alternative to the governing Parti socialiste. These attempts, however, have so far ended in relative failure.

The Coordination de l'Opposition Sénégalaise Unie and the Front d'Action Anti-Impérialiste

In 1978, during the Senghorian era of "guided democracy," six clandestine parties formed the Coordination de l'opposition sénégalaise unie (COSU) to press their demands for unlimited pluralism and full democratic rights. COSU was dominated by Mamadou Dia and his AND-SOPI group, which eventually crystallized in 1981 as the Mouvement démocratique populaire (MDP). It was also comprised of AND–JEF/MRDN, the Organisation démocratique prolétarienne (ODP), the LD/MPT, the PAI-Sénégal (which upon its legalization in 1981 became the PIT-S), and the Union pour la démocratie populaire (UDP). The main objective of COSU was the expansion of democratic rights through the legalization of unlimited pluralism. In addition, COSU became the vehicle for radical criticism of Senghor's regime, which it accused of being despotic, neocolonial, and corrupt.

With the coming of unlimited pluralism in 1981, COSU lost its fundamental political cause to the extent that the parties that comprised it were all legalized. This contributed to the fragmentation of an opposition that failed to develop a unified and effective programmatic alternative to the governing Parti socialiste during the elections of 1983. Even though the eight parties—the Ligue communiste des travailleurs, the LD/MPT, the MDP, the PIT-S, the PPS, the PAI, the UDP, and the PDS—signed a *plate-forme d'unité d'action des partis de l'opposition* that identified the government as the source of the masses' sufferings and miseries, and called for massive social change in a program of national renewal, the *plate-forme* failed to prevent the dissipation and the division of the opposition's forces.

These divisions were symbolized by the opposition's incapacity to settle on a common presidential candidate. The leaders of four parties of the opposition competed in the presidential elections: Abdoulaye Wade of the PDS, Mamadou Dia of the MDP, Oumar Wone of the PPS, and Majhemout Diop of the PAI. While the LCT, UDP, and LD/MPT supported Dia, the PIT-S Wade, and the OST Diop, these alliances were much too weak to challenge the candidacy of President Diouf. Thus, the *plate-forme* never came together as a meaningful, coherent, and unified alternative; it had dissolved in the face of personal and ideological differences.

The failure of the *plate-forme* did not, however, prevent the opposition from joining forces in an attempt to reverse the results of the elections, which it considered fraudulent. In March 1983, a *Déclaration des partis de l'opposition à l'issue de la mascarade électorale du 27 février 1983* was signed by eleven parties, those which had composed the *plate-forme*, the OST, RND, and MRS. Thus was formed the Cadre des 11, which the press dubbed the "Front du refus." The Front rejected the elections as scandalous and farcical, and it called for a plan of popular resistance against the government. The plan of resistance was to oppose "the confiscation of power by"

1. Rejecting both the results of the elections and the illegitimate government that such elections entailed
2. Demanding new, free, and democratic elections
3. Ending the exploitation of the popular masses through the radicalization of the social and political struggles against the neocolonialist regime and its servile unions
4. Intensifying the struggle for the defense, consolidation, and expansion of democratic and unionist freedoms
5. Strengthening the unity of combat by all the democratic and

anti-imperialist forces.[49]

This plan of resistance, however, never truly materialized, as new elections failed to take place and as the Front du refus itself slowly disintegrated; by April of 1983, the Front regrouped with only eight parties—AND–JEF/MRDN, LCT, LD/MPT, MDP, OST, PAI, PPS, and UDP—which condemned the "*plans anti-sociaux* of the *régime néocolonial PS.*"[50] Finally, by May of the same year, the Front was down to six parties—AND-JEF/MRDN, LCT, MDP, PAI, PPS, and UDP—which signed a new declaration opposing the government-sponsored revision of electoral lists. Thus, confronted with the intransigence of the Parti socialiste and the relative apathy of the masses, the opposition's wishes for unity quickly dissolved.

The opposition knew, however, that its hopes of capturing power from the PS depended on its capacity to present itself as a unified political bloc; however difficult and transitory they may have been in the past, political alliances remained a matter of survival for the opposition. This reality explains the emergence of the Front d'action anti-imperialiste—a regrouping of the LCT, MDP, PAI, and the PPS—which was formed in August 1983 to reject what it termed the *coup d'état électoral du 17 février 1983*. The Front, which identified itself as the heir of the COSU, was constituted to put an end to the *régime PS et à la domination étrangère*. It called for

> the organization of free and democratic elections for the national assembly, and for a government responsible to this assembly... charged with implementing a new policy of a break with imperialist and neocolonialist domination.[51]

Similar demands emerged from a joint declaration of the signatories of the Front, UDP, and LD/MPT. This declaration rejected President Diouf's appeals for a national consensus and a *sursaut national* as self-serving and cynical. It saw in the appeals a strategy for neutralizing and curbing the opposition's resistance to unpopular and neocolonial policies, and saw that they were to "create the necessary political balance of power to manage the crisis, to make sacrifices acceptable, and to stifle popular discontent."[52]

The Front, as well as the other ventures in common of the opposition, failed to gain the active support of the PDS—the largest nongovernment party. This failure partly explains the relative inefficiency of the opposition's resistance to the policies and programs of the ruling Parti socialiste. In July of 1985, however, the PDS finally decided to join forces with five other parties in the Alliance démocratique sénégalaise (ADS).

The Alliance Démocratique Sénégalaise

The Alliance démocratique sénégalaise organized the PDS, LCT, AND–JEF/MRDN, LD/MPT, OST, and UDP into a new opposition bloc.   It was the inclusion of the PDS that differentiated the ADS from its predecessors. The PDS, which had previously eschewed participation in the ventures of the opposition, finally realized that by itself it could not seriously challenge the PS. As its secretary general, Abdoulaye Wade, explained:

> You will observe that, with the exception of the common meeting of March 13, 1983, of eleven political parties to protest against the fraudulent elections of February 1983, the PDS has never joined an alliance of the parties of the opposition.... The government, until now, has tried hard to separate the PDS from the rest of the opposition....
> Together, the parties forming the ADS have succeeded in overcoming all the obstacles put in their way ... by the deceptive maneuvers of the PS and the government. An objective analysis has led us to the identification of real and fundamental convergences on which rest the foundation of our union.[53]

This union rests on the opposition in common by the members of the ADS to the policies and objectives of the government.   In its *Plate-forme d'unité d'action*, the ADS condemns vigorously the Parti socialiste's destatization of the economy, as well as its orthodox monetarist program of austerity. Moreover, the ADS placed full responsibility on the government for what it described as Senegal's most profound historical crisis, which was not only material, but also cultural, social, and political:

> The crisis that Senegal is experiencing is not conjunctural but structural. The existing system within which the crisis is taking place prevents all possibilities of national development.... It dramatically aggravates the process of the development of underdevelopment.... Discredited, weakened, and isolated by

massive popular defiance to its policies of electoral fraud, antidemocratic maneuvers, and social impoverishment, the government is now faced with a shrinking political and social base. This, in turn, has plunged it into utter disarray and forced it to rely systematically on violence, the only weapon available to an illegitimate regime.[54]

This sweeping condemnation of the government was accompanied by a plan of action that promised a political fight for improving the living standards of of the Senegalese masses, as well as for creating new jobs and increasing the minimum wage. It finally proposed a program of mobilization of national and international public opinion to attract attention to what it described as the "caractère dangereux de la politique du pouvoir."[55]

It remains to be seen if the ADS will be more successful in its endeavors than its many predecessors. Although it has enlisted the active support of the PDS, it has yet to enlarge its political base in other important sectors of the opposition. Also, the emergence of the ADS induced a crisis within the PDS as three of its young "rising stars" condemned the leadership of Wade for, among other things, entering into an alliance with "adventurous" left-wing parties. Although the crisis ended in the expulsion of the "gang of three" and thus was rapidly resolved in favor of Wade's forces, it indicated the tensions and vicissitudes besetting the ADS.[56] Indeed, in spite of certain convergences, the parties of the ADS have significant ideological and strategic differences that may ultimately paralyze action and engender divisions; the ADS is far from representing a coherent, viable, and unified alternative to the government.

Finally, even if the ADS were to surmount these difficulties and challenges, it would inevitably confront powerful opposition by the state. This opposition materialized in the government's legalistic maneuvres to portray the ADS as an illegal entity liable to banishment until and unless the parties belonging to it fused themselves into a single political party to gain proper legal status.[57] Although these legalistic maneuvers failed to the extent that the ADS continued to exist as a common front, they symbolized the fact that the law could be used and manipulated by the state to impose silence on the opposition. This, however, is not an exceptional peculiarity of the Senegalese political system, it is inherent in the structures of all state-societies. As Nicos

Poulantzas points out:

> The state often transgresses law-rules of its own making by
> acting without reference to the law, but also by acting directly
> against it.... This is called the higher interests of the State (raison
> d'Etat)—which, strictly speaking, entails both that legality is
> always compensated by illegalities 'on the side,' and that the state
> illegality is always inscribed in the legality which it institutes....
> Every juridical system includes illegality in the additional sense
> that gaps, blanks or 'loopholes' form an integral part of its
> discourse. It is a question here not merely of oversights or
> blindspots arising out of the ideological operation of concealment
> underlying the legal order, but of express devices that allow the
> law to be breached.... Not only does illegality often enter into the
> law, but illegality and legality are themselves part of one and the
> same institutional structure.[58]

Thus, at this juncture, the democratic and legalistic constraints of the Senegalese passive revolution might impose hard
limits on the ADS' capacity to effect the changes and
transformations that it has promised. These limits, however,
are not all there are in the Senegalese political system. This
system, as well as its laws, reflects the relation of forces
existing between conflicting groups and classes; it solidifies the
gains and losses of these groups and classes. To quote
Poulantzas again:

> Law does not only deceive and conceal, nor does it merely
> repress people by compelling or forbidding them to act. It also
> recognizes and sanctions certain real rights of the dominated
> classes (even though, of course, these rights are invested in the
> dominant ideology, and are far from corresponding in practice to
> their judicial form); and it has inscribed within it the material
> concessions imposed on the dominant classes by popular
> struggle.[59]

Similarly, Senegal's passive revolution represents a
concession of the PS/state to the democratic pressures exercized
by the opposition in the late 1960s and afterward: it legalized and
legitimated dissent within the confine of a liberal democracy. It
is true that it was effected as a means of curbing the
radicalization of the subaltern classes, but it provided a certain
room for maneuver and a certain breathing space for
progressive forces to offer radical political alternatives,
however vague, to the existing reality of a severe peripheral
capitalist crisis.

This is not to say that these alternatives will materialize in the near future, but to emphasize that the passive revolution may unleash a dialectic of change that may transgress the perimeters of liberal democracy. Seen in this light, the reforms brought about by the passive revolution, however limited they may be, cannot be dismissed as mere sham: they represent a new political configuration that simultaneously creates opportunities and dangers. They form a basis on which progressive forces can further the expansion of democratic rights, but they are also fragile and subject to sudden death.

The decision to participate in the political and electoral process unleashes a dialectical process that simultaneously creates the potential for and contributes to the closure of radical social alternatives. To a considerable degree, the Senegalese parties advocating the socialist transformation of their society are all facing the antinomies that have characterized the historical development of social democracy. Adam Przeworski explains the antirevolutionary and reformist nature of these antinomies:

> Participation in electoral politics is necessary if the movement for socialism is to find mass support among workers, yet this participation seems to obstruct the attainment of final goals. Working for today and working toward tomorrow appear as contrasting horns of a dilemma....
>
> To win votes of people other than workers, particularly the petty bourgeoisie, to form alliances and coalitions, to administer the government in the interest of workers, a party cannot appear to be 'irresponsible,' to give any indication of being less than whole-hearted about its commitment to the rules and the limits of the parliamentary game. At times the party must even restrain its own followers from actions that would jeopardize electoral progress. Moreover, a party oriented toward partial improvements, a party in which leader-representatives lead a petty bourgeois life style, a party that for years has shied away from the streets cannot 'pour through the hole in the trenches' ... even when this opening is forged by a crisis.[60]

This dilemma confronting all revolutionaries operating in bourgeois parliamentarian democracies is even more acute in Senegal where reformism stems not only from the dialectics of the electoral process, but also from the constraining range of economic choices opened to its monocrop, dependent, and peripheral capitalism. In societies such as Senegal's, the possibilities for the expansion of democratic practices, let alone for revolutionary transformations, just happen to be extremely limited. The Senegalese opposition is therefore facing the prospects of cooptation, reformism, and electoralism. Any other choice might condemn it to perpetual electoral defeats, or banishment to the obscure ghetto of clandestinity and illegality. This is not to say that a revolutionary alternative is impossible, but that the passive revolution has rendered it highly unlikely. But it is not just revolution that is unlikely; moderate policies in the direction of greater social justice are also difficult to implement in a society like Senegal's where conditions of severe material scarcity prevail, and where the class-ridden character of bourgeois social relations imposes the most drastic and harshest constraints on the already limited reformist reach of liberal democracy. The issue of the democratic limits of liberal democracy is therefore raised. It constitutes the subject of the next chapter.

Notes

1. Abdou Diouf, *Rapport de Politique Générale: Le PS, Moteur du Sursaut National*, Dakar: Publications du Parti Socialiste, 1984, 5–6 (my translation).

2. Abdou Diouf, *Le Sursaut National avec Abdou Diouf*, Dakar: Publications du Parti Socialiste, no date, 28–33 (my translation).

3. Abdou Diouf, *Rapport de Politique Générale: Le PS, Moteur du Sursaut National*, 21.

4. Gerti Hesseling, *Histoire Politique du Sénégal*, Paris: Karthala, 1985, 298–299.

5. Abdou Diouf, "Message à l'Occasion de la Fête Nationale du 4 Avril 1983," *Revue des Institutions Politiques et Administratives du Sénégal*, Nos. 6/7 (janvier–juin 1983): 3–4 (my translation).

6. Abdou Diouf, *Rapport de Politique Générale: Le PS, Moteur du Sursaut National*, 28–29 (my translation).

7. Ibid., 13–18.

8. Gerti Hesseling, Histoire Politique du Sénégal, 287–289.

9. Mar Fall, "Le Multipartisme et l'Union Nationale au Sénégal?" *Le Mois en Afrique*, Nos. 217–218 (1985): 35–37.

10. Ibid., 36.

11. Abdou Diouf, *Rapport Introductif*, Dakar: Conseil National du Parti Socialiste, 11 mai 1985, 12 (my translation).

12. *Le Soleil*, 21 mai 1985, 2 (my translation).

13. *Le Soleil*, 30 mai 1985, 10.

14. Richard Sandbrook, *The Politics of Basic Needs: Urban Aspects of Assaulting Poverty in Africa*, Toronto: University of Toronto Press, 1982, 239–240.

15. Pathé Diagne, *Sénégal: Crise Economique et Sociale et Devenir de la Démocratie*, Dakar: Sankore, 1984, 31 (my translation).

16. Abdoulaye Wade, "Notre Doctrine du Travaillisme," *Revue des Institutions Politiques et Aministratives du Sénégal*, No. 5, (octobre–décembre 1982): 577–578 (my translation).

17. Abdoulaye Wade, "La Doctrine Economique du Mouridisme," *Annales Africaines* (Faculté de Droit et des Sciences Economiques de l'Université de Dakar), 1967, 175–208.

18. Parti Démocratique Sénégalais, *Programme Fondamental du Socialisme-Travailliste*, quoted as cited in *Revue des Institutions Politiques et Administratives du Sénégal*, No. 5, (octobre–décembre 1982): 559, (my translation).

19. Abdoulaye Wade, "Le Plan de Redressement Economique du Parti Démocratique Sénégalais," *Revue des Institutions Politiques et Administratives du Sénégal*, No. 5, (octobre–décembre 1982): 588–589 (my translation).

20. Ibid., 590.

21. Personal interviews with Abdoulaye Wade, April 30 and May 7, 1985.

22. Abdoulaye Wade, "Il Faut Sauver La Patrie," *Takusaan*, No. 39, (juillet 1983), 6–15 (my translation).

23. Personal interviews with Abdoulaye Wade.

24. Wade, "Il Faut Sauver La Patrie," 15.

25. Diagne, *Sénégal: Crise Economique et Sociale et Devenir de la Démocratie*, 43–44 (my translation).

26. AND–JEF, "Programme de AND–JEF," *Revue des Institutions Politiques et Administratives du Sénégal* , No. 5 (octobre–décembre 1982): 676 (my translation).

27. Ibid.

28. Ibid., 677.

29. Diagne, *Sénégal: Crise Economique et Sociale et Devenir de la Démocratie*, 56–58; Jacques Mariel Nzouankeu, *Les Partis Politiques Sénégalais*, Dakar: Editions Claireafrique, 1984, 78–83.

30. Landing Savane, *La Situation Economique du Sénégal et le FMI*, Dakar: AND–JEF/MRDN, 1981, 3–13 (my translation).

31. Parti Africain de l'Indépendance, "Programme du Parti Africain de l'Indépendance," *Revue des Institutions Politiques et Administratives du Sénégal*, No. 5 (octobre–décembre 1982): 754 (my translation).

32. Ibid., 760.

33. Majhemout Diop, personal communication to the author, May 13, 1985, 2 (my translation).

34. Ibid.

35. Nzouankeu, *Les Partis Politiques Sénégalais*, 99–118.

36. Ligue Démocratique/Mouvement pour le Parti du Travail, "Projet de Programme de la Ligue Démocratique/Mouvement pour le Parti du Travail," *Revue des Institutions Politiques et Administratives du Sénégal* , (octobre–décembre 1982): 795 (my translation).

37. Ibid., 796.

38. Ibid., 798.

39. Ibid.

40. Ibid., 797.

41. Ibid.

42. Ibid., 801–802.

43. Ibid., 807.

44. Ibid.

45. Personal interview with Abdoulaye Bathily, November 13, 1985.

46. PAI–SENEGAL, "Plate-forme d'Action de Lutte Présentée par le Comité Central du PAI–SENEGAL," *Revue des Institutions Politiques et Administratives du Sénégal*, No. 5, (octobre–décembre 1982): 839 (my translation).

47. PAI–SENEGAL, "Le Concept de Révolution Nationale et Démocratique," *Revue des Institutions Politiques et Administratives du Sénégal*, No. 5, (octobre–décembre 1982): 842–843 (my translation).

48. Diagne, *Sénégal: Crise Economique et Sociale et Devenir de la Démocratie*, 59–60 (my translation).

49. "Déclaration des Partis de l'Opposition à l'Issue de la Mascarade Electorale du 27 Février 1983," *Revue des Institutions Politiques et Administratives du Sénégal*, Nos. 6–7, (janvier–juin 1983): 360 (my translation).

50. "Déclaration des Partis de l'Opposition," *Revue des Institutions Politiques et Administratives du Sénégal*, Nos. 6–7, (janvier–juin 1983): 362.

51. Suxxali Reew Mi (Front d'Action Anti-Impérialiste), "Communiqué," *Revue des Institutions Politiques et Administratives du Sénégal*, No. 8, (octobre–décembre 1983): 784 (my translation).

52. Ibid., 786.

53. Abdoulaye Wade, cited as quoted in *Le Démocrate* , No. 32, (juillet 1985), 2 (my translation).

54. *Plate-forme d'Unité d'Action l'Alliance Démocratique Sénégalaise*, flyer, 1985 (my translation).

55. Ibid.

56. *Le Démocrate*, No. 34, (octobre–novembre 1985).

57. *Le Démocrate*, No. 33, (août–septembre 1985), 6.

58. Nicos Poulantzas, *State, Power, Socialism* , London: Verso Edition, 1980, 84–85.

59. Ibid., 84.

60. Adam Przeworski, "Social Democracy as Historical Phenomenon," *New Left Review*, No. 122, (July–August 1980), 28–31.

6

Epilogue: Passive Revolution and Liberal Democracy

In the previous chapters I have argued that the passive revolution that the Senegalese ruling class effected responded to internal, as well as external, factors. It contributed to a greater rationalization of domestic political practices, it initiated the transformation of the soft state into an integral state, and it coopted the opposition into the new liberal democratic system of participation and representation. Thus, the passive revolution partially resolved the organic crisis that had paralyzed the political economy. In addition, it solidified and sought to restructure the alliance between the managers of the state and the agents of foreign capital.

Hence, the explanatory framework provided by the passive revolution model, like the dependent-Marxist paradigm, takes into consideration the organic crisis of peripheral capitalism, but it does so within the context of the formative efforts of the ruling class. As such, it preserves the autonomy of the political domain and the domestic class struggles without negating the impact of the processes of capitalist accumulation on a world scale. Thus, in the passive revolution model there is no inevitability; there are opportunities for different histories and political forms, but there are, however, powerful structures that restrict action to definite parameters. To construct a paradigm that would elucidate events otherwise would leave unexplained the fact that, upon experiencing similar contradictions and processes, peripheral societies respond differently and create different regimes and institutions.

The extent to which Senegal evolved into a liberal democracy is an indication that the requirements of the accumulation of capital in the periphery can be met without necessarily resorting to the barbarism of the "specialists of coercion." This symbolizes also the success of a politically talented ruling class. Indeed, this ruling class simultaneously preserved its domination over the "many" while replacing its entrenched authoritarianism with a liberal democracy. That the rise of liberal democracy in Senegal has not fundamentally altered the relations of power is an indication of the obdurate democratic limits of liberal democracy itself. But, it is also true that, however obdurate these limits may be, they are more bearable to the working classes than the brutally repressive rule of the specialists of coercion.

The Exportability and Limitations of Senegal's "Passive Revolution"

Is Senegal Unique?

The success of Senegal's passive revolution raises the question of its exportability to other dependent nations. In other words, can these nations effect a similar passive revolution in order to escape from the unmitigated evil of coercive authoritarianism that stems from the organic crisis of peripheral capitalism? For a variety of historical and political reasons, it appears that the Senegalese experience is unique and unlikely to be repeated in other parts of the periphery.

Senegal's own colonial history—in contradistinction to that of the periphery in general—imparted to its politics a certain commitment to the values of liberal democracy. Unlike most colonies, Senegal, and in particular its urban areas, or the "four communes," enjoyed a relatively enlightened pattern of French imperial domination. As Wesley Johnson put it, "The Senegalese case was probably unique ... because in the Four Communes political activity was allowed rather than being proscribed."[1] In fact, the four communes implanted in the Senegalese terrain a tradition of competitive and interracial electoral politics. It is true that it was a tradition of an elite, but it nonetheless contributed to the rise of African mass politics.[2] Thus, in contrast to most peripheral nations, Senegal experienced a rather democratic form of imperial domination, and this decisively impinged on its postcolonial politics.

Upon obtaining independence in 1960, Senegal was

characterized by an intensely competitive political system, as Senghor's UPS never was able to impose monopolistic hegemony over opposing parties. The ambiguity of the UPS's struggle against French colonialism created the necessary terrain for deep divisions in the Senegalese political class.[3] Such divisions were reinforced by the pluralist tradition of the four communes, as well as by new ideological differences. This competitive and pluralist legacy continually haunted Senghor's authoritarian ascendancy. Indeed, it took Senghor four years of ruthless princely rule to establish his presidential absolutism, which he eventually undid in 1976. In this sense, the entrenched electoral tradition of competitive politics imposed certain limitations to authoritarianism and contributed to the success of the "passive revolution."

Such success was also a consequence of Senghor's mastery of princely rule itself. Indeed, as Jean-Pierre Ndiaye points out, Senghor's political experience and intelligence had given him a weapon that was

> a supple and effective method that moves situations and people into his own orbit, and that attracts them into his own terrain without his ever losing control. Yet, he is also a man of culture and a poet: the antithesis of *homo politicus*. His personality is therefore double, ambiguous, complex.... If his soul were sincere, the intelligence of his spirit was inhabited, like that of any fighter, by agility and cunning.[4]

Moreover, Senghor's worldwide cultural status facilitated his departure from the presidency and thus the institutionalization of the passive revolution, as he knew that the end of his political life would send him neither to exile nor oblivion, but to his literary apotheosis. Senghor the poet was indeed unique among African and most other political leaders in that he could step down from the Senegalese presidency to ascend into the ranks of *les immortels* of the French Academy. In this perspective, Senghor, the man of letters, could end his political career without any loss of prestige and grandeur to pursue a rewarding romance with culture. Finally, Senghor assured his place in history by becoming the first African president to relinquish voluntarily and peacefully the reigns of power. Politics for the former president had represented a "long parenthesis" from which he finally extricated himself and on which he decided to remain politely silent. Senghor could turn his intellectual energies to his theme of predilection—*la civilisation de l'universel*. He was now in the process of writing *De la négritude à la civilisation*, a major theoretical synthesis of his philosophical vision.[5]

Therefore, Senghor's poetic and Machiavellian attributes were important in the making of Senegal's passive revolution. By assuring a peaceful transition of power and the institutionalization of princely rule, they contributed to changing things so that they could remain the same. They helped integrate the opposition into the existing structures of power and rendered impotent the challenge of potentially revolutionary forces. That President Diouf exercised these same Machiavellian attributes of princely rule could only reinforce and indeed consolidate the passive revolution. In this sense, the success of this passive revolution has greatly depended on the exceptional political talents of Senegal's two princes. As such, the democratization of Senegal is not easily duplicable elsewhere.

The Senegalese passive revolution, however, comes from much more than mere talented political leadership; it is also a product of structural factors. It was effected, above all, because the threat of the left was incoherent and diffuse and, because of that, manageable.[6] Neither the proletariat nor the peasantry was mobilized in a revolutionary party. The threat of the left was, in fact, nothing more than a general and systemic social malaise. Furthermore, the Senegalese ruling class could itself afford a democratization because it was conducted within certain bounds that never went beyond the existing alignments of class power and inequalities. And, finally, if these alignments were to be challenged or threatened, they could always be reestablished by the "French praetorian guard [which was] encamped on the perimeter of Senegal's only international airport."[7]

To this extent, the circumstances characterizing Senegal's passive revolution seem to be exceptional. Not only did Senegal enjoy a different colonial history in the opportunities that it offered for liberal democratic practices, but it also came under the postcolonial presidentialism of two exeptional rulers who exercised their statecraft in the most Machiavellian sense. In addition, the period of Senghorian authoritarianism implanted the structures of dependent capitalism so deeply into the Senegalese terrain that nothing short of revolution could displace them. The passive revolution that crystallized as a liberal democracy represented, therefore, the institutionalization and consolidation of these structures.

This raises the question of whether other peripheral societies can, after years of authoritarian implantation of dependent capitalism, effect a passive revolution à la Sénégalaise. Can they abandon dictatorial and/or military rule and bring in a liberal democratic framework? In short, is Senegal's passive revolution announcing a generalized pattern of political "decompression" or is it an exceptional phenomenon?

On the one hand, there seems to be a tendency toward liberalization in certain parts of the periphery and in Latin America in particular, although Africa appears to be unaffected.[8] This tendency may reflect the increasing popular challenges to the brutality and austerity that a dependent capitalism based on export promotion entails. It may also stem from the ruling class's renewed interest in a policy of import substitution whose reliance on the enlargement of the domestic market would require a more egalitarian distribution of wealth. This, in turn, would necessitate a political realignment bent on creating more democratic and popular forms of governance. Passive revolutions would be the means to that end.[9]

On the other hand, such passive revolutions may not entail any restructuring of dependent capitalism, but, on the contrary, may legitimize this very type of (under)development. André Gunder Frank points out that

> this apparent democratization is simply the institutionalization of the new model of economic growth based on export promotion. It was necessary to have very severe political repression as a midwife to institute this new model; but once the model is in place and more or less working, it is possible to ease off a bit on the political repression. Then, indeed, it is not only possible, but it becomes politically necessary and desirable to get a wider social base for the political regime and to institute a kind of limited political democracy by handing over the government from military to civilian rule. But these political modifications would not be made in order to overturn the present economic order and again to promote import substitution, let alone so-called noncapitalist growth or some variety of "socialism." Instead, this supposed redemocratization would be to maintain and to institutionalize the new insertion of the Third World in the international division of labor as low-wage producers during the present world economic crisis.[10]

This process of redemocratization, however, does not seem to represent the general political tendency of peripheral societies. Rather, most peripheral ruling classes lack the maturity, security, and assurance required for allowing passive revolutions. They fear that such revolutions might open up a Pandora's box and be particularly hazardous to their privileges and interests. Structuring a strategy of economic growth around policies of export promotion while attempting to absorb new classes into a liberal system of dissent and opposition may ultimately unleash uncontrollable forces. Thus, instead of institutionalizing the existing patterns of wealth, privilege, and power, a passive revolution might well threaten their very roots.

Senegal's experience symbolizes the hegemonic capacities of its ruling class, and it is difficult to see—in spite of a few exceptions—how it can be extended throughout the periphery and Africa in particular. The external and domestic circumstances characterizing the crisis of dependent capitalism are more likely to further dictatorship, repression, and martial law than passive revolutions and liberal democracies. Indeed, power holders are generally apprehensive about passive revolutions because they fear that far from curbing discontent they might enhance opposition and further raise popular expectations.

Such apprehension, however, may be misguided since passive revolutions have historically been the sine qua non of the continued rule of the bourgeoisie. Although it would be wrong to see in passive revolutions nothing more than mere sham, it is safe to say that they have been inspired by the ruling circles' commitment to preserve the existing mode of social reproduction. They have not drastically altered the ugly realities of poverty, exploitation, and inequality; in fact, they have contributed to their legitimation. It is in this perspective that the Senegalese process of democratization must be understood.

Passive revolutions are processes of integration of subordinate classes into political and economic structures that protect and serve the fundamental interests of the dominant classes. While they are generally initiated as a result of popular resistance against the privileges and powers of the ruling class, it is the ruling class itself that channels them into forms of representation appropriate to its continued domination. This is not to say that the ruling class is always contented with the processes unfolding from the making of passive revolutions, but rather that such processes are necessary for the maintenance of its power. These processes assure the integration of the popular masses into a democratized framework of bourgeois governance.

The Democratic Limitations of Liberal Democracy

The passive revolution of Senegal has therefore preserved the domination of the few over the many, and maintained the relative impotence of the masses over the means of production and the organs of state power. It has, however, opened certain opportunities for the expansion of democracy and the assertion of greater popular control; and the acceptance of different political parties anchored in different social classes and accepting different class discourses has exploded the old myth of classless Africa expounded by Senghor himself and the ideologists of African socialism.[11] In that light, Senegal has entered the era of genuine class politics and, as such, the question of a real radical political alternative has been plainly put.   Paradoxically, though, class politics in bourgeois parliamentarian forms of representation and elections implies a decisive deemphasis of class as a mode of mobilization and struggle. As Przeworski has remarked:

> The rules of the democratic game, while universal and at times fair, show no compassion.... The combination of minority status with majority rule constitutes the historical condition under which socialists have to act. This objective condition imposes upon socialists ... a choice: socialists must choose between a party homogeneous in its class appeal, but sentenced to perpetual electoral defeats, and a party that struggles for electoral success at the cost of diluting its class character.[12]

Thus, when revolutionary socialist parties have chosen to participate in the democratic practices of bourgeois parliamentarism they are inevitably drawn into compromises and alliances that dilute the importance of class. Again, as Przeworski has put it:

> By broadening their appeal to the 'masses,' social democrats weaken the general salience of class as a determinant of the political behaviour of individuals.... When social democratic parties become parties 'of the entire nation,' they reinforce the vision of politics as a process of defining the collective welfare of 'all members of the society.' Politics, once again, is defined

in the dimension individual-nation, not in terms of class.[13]

The revolutionary parties of Senegal are thus confronting the dilemma of their social democratization. Whether they will avoid the pitfalls of reformism that this entails has yet to be determined by the future of Senegalese politics. Yet, if historical experience is any guide, then the journey to socialism will be hard and full of compromising detours; and, if they succeed in their final goals through the electoral road of bourgeois parliamentarism, they will in all likelihood be confronted with a challenge by powerful reactionary forces. In this instance, class politics may become a ferocious struggle for power instead of a gentlemanly process of compromises. Really, the question is would the Senegalese ruling class be prepared to accept electoral defeat and relinquish its hegemony without resorting to force or a preemptive coup; that is, would it tolerate the ascendancy of revolutionary forces and preserve its constitutional rectitude? If the history of Senegal—and, for that matter, of all class societies—is any indication, it would be absurd to expect a peaceful surrender of the ruling classes, and, in this sense, a revolutionary alternative is indeed an impossibility.

In addition, because the Parti socialiste has come to embody the state and has therefore politicized the vast bureaucratic apparatus, it has created multiple social fortresses bent on preserving the status quo and aborting any alternative. This type of politicization, as Nicos Poulantzas has remarked in a different context, generates the following important phenomena:

> the restricted circulation of political personnel; the emergence of multiform corporatist interests based on the holding of posts; the distribution of state sinecures; the diversion of public funds for party aims; the trading in influence between dominant party and State; and the subservience of that party to big business. Although these have always been features of bourgeois States, they are now assuming quite prodigious dimensions; and although they are doubtless secondary phenomena, they considerably heighten the resistance of the dominant party-State to democratic alternatives. Leaving aside the possible dangers for the dominant classes themselves, loss of governmental power would both strip away a whole series of material privileges and threaten with disintegration a party whose importance rests precisely with its role in the State.[14]

Thus, it is not only a real radical political alternative that is endangered by the ruling class's determination to preserve its status, but the possibility of a mere alternation of power might well unleash authoritarian measures. The electoral victory of a party other than a socialist party, while not necessarily challenging the fundamental structures of the existing system, would nonetheless threaten the narrow corporate interests of important bureaucratic groups since this party would inevitably seek to impose its own personalistic network of patron-client relationships. Even if, historically, alternations of power in liberal democracies have been associated with the rise of reformist politics within the parameters of existing bourgeois social relations rather than with the revolutionary socialist transformation of society, the danger of ruling class repression always exists.[15]

When all of this and more has been said about the Senegalese passive revolution, it remains the case that it embodies, to a large extent, the guarantee for the established order and the death of fundamental change. The passive revolution resulted more from the ruling class's determined opposition to massive structural changes in the political and economic repartition of power than from an organized popular demand for such repartition. It stemmed more from the efforts of the ruling class to preempt and moderate the rise of a popular insurrectionary will than from any coherent peasant and proletarian threat to the existing order. Hence, the passive revolution blunted the edge of apprehended and probable class confrontations by smoothing over the integration of the masses into an "expanded state."

The concept of an expanded state derives from Gramsci's idea that to exercise hegemony over subaltern classes, a ruling class must relinquish some of its immediate interests and privileges. As Gramsci explains:

It is true that the State is seen as the organ of one particular group, destined to create favourable conditions for the latter's maximum expansion. But the development and expansion of the particular group are conceived of, and presented, as being the motor force of a universal expansion, of a development of all the 'national' energies. In other words, the dominant group is coordinated concretely with the general interests of the subordinate groups, and the life of the State is conceived of as a continuous process of formation and superseding of unstable equilibria (on the juridical plane) between the interests of the fundamental group and those of the subordinate groups—equilibria in which the interests of the dominant group prevail, but only up to a certain point, i.e., stopping short of narrowly corporate economic interest.[16]

Hegemony requires the "expansion" of the state whereby potential allies and even antagonistic elements are gradually absorbed into the institutions of that state. But precisely because the Senegalese expansion occured as a passive revolution it imposed obdurate limitations to democratic practice; it could not transcend the parameters of liberal democracy. Put another way, the democratic franchise and unlimited political pluralism came as late additions to the dependent capitalist society presided over by Senghor and Diouf. While they transformed the authoritarian state into a liberal state, they did not in any way threaten the fundamental structures of that society; in fact, they became the fulfillment of Senegalese dependent capitalism.

The implantation of liberal democracy in Senegal has blunted the edge of potential class confrontations by moderating and smoothing over the opposition. It has facilitated the imposition of the material sacrifices required for the functioning of dependent capitalism by imparting to them the quality of absolute necessities for the survival and consolidation of liberal democracy itself. In other words, the fresh memory of authoritarianism has contributed to the developmnent of a generalized political pragmatism and gradualism, and thus subordinated the commitment to fundamental structural change to the preservation of the existing system of power and privilege. By absorbing revolutionary and opposition movements into its constitutional and legal political structure, the Senegalese form of liberal democracy has imposed rigid limitations on these movements' mode of operation. It has, paradoxically, curbed the intensity of opposition, reduced the number of alternatives, and blurred the horizon of options. In other words, it is a successful liberal democracy. For as Joseph Schumpeter emphasized, the maintenance and consolidation of a liberal democracy presuppose that "the effective range of political decision should not be extended too far ... democracy does not require that every function of the state be subject to its political method."[17]

However limited and constrained the passive revolution may have been, it embodied nonetheless the essence of a liberal democracy: it granted to the citizenry the fundamental legal freedoms of speech, association, and participation, and it established a practice of competitive elections in a system of unlimited pluralism. These rights by themselves do not amount to the constitution of a truly "democratic society," and they are quite compatible with the persistence of great material inequalities, massive poverty, and class exploitation. One of its defenders honestly admits that

> [liberal] democracy does not necessarily assure even a reasonable approximation of what we would call a democratic society, a society with considerable equality of opportunity in all spheres, including social equality, as well as opportunity to formulate political alternatives and mobilize the electorate for them.[18]

Senegal's democracy, like any other bourgeois liberal democracy, is "crippled by its class limitations and under constant threat of further and drastic impairment by conservative forces, never more so than in an epoch of permanent and severe crisis."[19]   Indeed, if Senegal's democratic experience is based on the relative hegemony of its ruling class, it is the armor of coercion that ultimately preserves it.[20] The element of consent is also a product of the structures of repression, even when these structures do not intrude directly into political society.   The hegemony of the ruling class is upheld by the legal compulsion of the state and thus by the continuous threat of force. This was clearly demonstrated when Abdoulaye Wade and Abdoulaye Bathily, the principal leaders of the Alliance démocratique sénégalaise and the respective secretaries general of the PDS and the LD–MPT, were imprisoned in August 1985 for several days for trying to organize in Dakar an antiapartheid meeting that had been banned by the governor of the region. Although all of them were eventually released by the departmental court of Dakar, which found them not guilty, the incident was a grim reminder of the constant threat of coercion.[21]

Thus, as Nicos Poulantzas argues:

> Even if violence is not concretized in the daily exercise of power as it used to be, it still, and indeed more than ever, occupies a determining position. For its very monopolization by the State induces forms of domination in which the numerous methods of establishing consent play the key role.... Violence-terror

always occupies a determining place—and not merely because it remains in reserve, coming into the open only in critical situations. State-monopolized physical violence permanently underlies the techniques of power and mechanisms of consent: it is inscribed in the web of disciplinary and ideological devices; and even when not directly exercised, it shapes the materiality of the social body upon which domination is brought to bear.[22]

This is particularly the case for Senegal where the weight of the authoritarianism of the past continuously haunts and shapes the opposition's behavior; to avoid a possible breakdown of liberal democracy and a return to authoritarianism, the opposition has accepted the "rules of the game" and moderated its demands for change. It is becoming a "loyal opposition" with a vested interest in the consolidation of liberal democracy.

In these circumstances, Senegal's new liberal democracy seems to be anchored in safe waters. This does not mean that it is bound to survive the persisting economic crisis and that it is immune to a potential military coup. In fact, it is confronting serious social, regional, and political challenges that may dislocate its new and fragile structures. The patterns of unequal development among the different sectors of society have created the conditions for ethnic divisions and confrontations. In this respect, the emergence in the southern region of Casamance of the separatist Mouvement des forces démocratiques de Casamance is an indication that these patterns of unequal development may threaten traditionally peaceful ethnic relations.[23]

The measures of austerity that have been implemented to resolve the economic crisis have also enhanced the potential for further social and ethnic disorders. These disorders may, in turn, reach such explosive levels that the possibility of a military coup should not be dismissed. It is true that the military in Senegal has a tradition of republicanism and subordination to civil authorities, but it is a tradition that may be hard put to survive an exacerbation of the continuing organic crisis. The Senegalese military sees its role as guardians of the public order and, accordingly, they may be forced to intervene if such order is endangered. As the chief of staff, General Joseph Louis Tavares Da Souza explained in an interview in *Le Soleil*:

When we see a country change governments or systems every two or three years, when we see a coup d'etat overthrow another coup d'etat time and time again, then I say that such armies are not true armies. They are the leaders of gangs fighting for power. An army does not let itself be dragged into taking power. When it is forced by circumstance to do so, it is certainly with the objective of creating order and reestablishing democracy. In any case, it is in this spirit that we have been educated, and it is in this spirit that we intend to educate our young soldiers.[24]

The dangers to the survival of Senegalese democracy are therefore real, but they seem far less significant than the structures of support maintaining it. On the one hand, democracy legitimates the rule of the powerholders without endangering their continued supremacy; on the other hand, it represents a safe ground, however narrow it may be, for political dissent and participation. The dictatorial and brutal context of African politics has enhanced the commitment of the country's entire political class to the value of liberal democracy and to the social order that it entails.[25] In spite of its obvious limitations and deficiencies, the coming of liberal democracy in Senegal has facilitated the organization of the popular sectors into power blocs and political parties capable of influencing the political agenda and altering society's collective fate. Because liberal democracy imposes certain important legal and cultural limitations on the repressive power of both the state and the ruling class, it inevitably generates popular means of resistance against enduring forms of exploitation, domination, and privilege.

While the coming of liberal democracy in Senegal has enhanced the legitimation of the powerholders, it has also unfolded a dynamic of reforms that may generate among subaltern classes a momemtum for more radical demands. There is obviously no guarantee that the greater political empowerment of these subaltern classes will engender processes of structural transformations in the economy and the social system. Such empowerment, however, makes these transformations more likely. The Senegalese passive revolution, whatever its shortcomings may be, is a concession by the powerholders since it curbs their authority and sets definite parameters to their policies. So, even though it was designed to mitigate the challenge of the masses, it offered them the possibility of taking the initiative and developing centers of relative political autonomy. As Ralph Miliband remarks:

It is nonsense to say ... that reform does not 'really' affect the 'ruling class.' The latter's members squeal much more than is usually warranted. But the squealing is on the other hand rather more than mere sham: the sense of being adversely affected and constrained is real; and this is quite often an accurate reflection of the concrete impact of this or that measure and action of the state.[26]

However crippled it may be, Senegal's democracy represents an important advance over the vast majority of peripheral, and in particular African, regimes where corruption and privilege rule with brute and dictatorial force. The civic freedoms that the Senegalese people have painfully won should neither be dismissed nor ignored; they constitute the arena in which will be waged the future struggles for the further expansion of democracy. The general elections of 1988 and the ways and means by which they will be held will indicate whether these struggles will translate into more vigorous participatory institutions and practices. They will represent one of the most crucial tests by which the long-term success of the Senegalese liberal democratic experiment is likely to depend. They will also demonstrate whether the Senegalese state is an *état d'exception* to the extent that, in peripheral societies, "the exceptional state is democracy, and the normal state is the regime of limited legitimacy."[27]

Be that as it may, Senegal's liberal democratic experiment represents a still fragile foundation on which more profound democratic values and practices may be erected. This is so because liberal democracy as a historical form of representation occupies only an underdeveloped region, and indeed the desert region of this vast continent that is Democracy. It remains to be seen whether Senegalese men and women will be able to travel beyond these desert boundaries and discover the uncharted territories of a truly democratic and socialist world.

Notes

1. Wesley Johnson, *The Emergence of Black Politics in Senegal*, Stanford: Stanford University Press, 1971, viii.
2. Ibid., 139–219.
3. Joseph Roger de Benoist, *L'Afrique Occidentale Française de 1944 à 1960*, Dakar: Les Nouvelles Editions Africaines, 1982, 103–128, 212–221, 321–337, 352–370, 401–408, 435–505.

4. Jean-Pierre Ndiaye, *Monde Noir et Destin Politique*, Dakar: Les Nouvelles Editions Africaines, 1976, 165 (my translation).

5. Personal interview with Léopold Sédar Senghor, November 11, 1985.

6. Ndiaye, *Monde Noir et Destin Politique*, 163–164.

7. Donal B. Cruise O'Brien, "Senegal," in John Dunn, ed., *West African States: Failure and Promise* , Cambridge: Cambridge University Press, 1978, 180–181.

8. Goran Therborn, "The Travail of Latin American Democracy," *New Left Review*, Nos. 113–114 (January–April 1979): 71–109.

9. André Gunder Frank, *Crisis: In the Third World*, New York: Holmes and Meier Publishers, 1981, 323–326.

10. Ibid., 325–326.

11. Irving Leonard Markovitz, *Léopold Sédar Senghor and the Politics of Négritude*, New York: Atheneum, 1969, 119–193. Julius Nyerere, *Freedom and Socialism*, London: Oxford University Press, 1968. Aristide Zolberg, *Creating Political Order*, Chicago: Rand McNally, 1966.

12. Adam Przeworski, "Social Democracy as a Historical Phenomenon," *New Left Review*, No. 122, (July–August 1980), 39.

13. Ibid., 42–43.

14. Nicos Poulantzas, *State, Power, Socialism* , London: Verso Edition, 1980, 235.

15. Ralph Miliband, *Marxism and Politics*, New York: Oxford University Press, 1977, 162–163.

16. Antonio Gramsci, *Selections from Prison Notebooks*, edited and translated by Quintin Hoare and Geoffrey Nowell Smith, London: Lawrence and Wishart, 1971, 182.

17. Joseph Schumpeter, *Capitalism, Socialism and Democracy*, 3rd. ed., New York: Harper Brothers, 1975, 291–292.

18. Juan Linz, *Crisis, Breakdown and Reequilibration*, Baltimore: The Johns Hopkins University Press, 1981, 97.

19. Miliband, *Marxism and Politics*, 189.

20. Gramsci, *Selections from Prison Notebooks*, 263.

21. *Le Soleil*, 28 août 1985; 29 août 1985; 30 août 1985; 31 août 1985.

22. Poulantzas, *State, Power, Socialism*, 80–81.

23. Gerti Hesseling, *Histoire Politique du Sénégal*, Paris: Karthala, 1985, 44–45.

24. *Le Soleil*, 22–23 septembre 1984, 5.

25. Howard French, "Diouf Faces Tough Tests," *Africa News*, Vol. 23, No. 21–22, 11–12.

26. Miliband, *Marxism and Politics*, 88.

27. Gilberto Mathias and Pierre Salama, *L'Etat Surdéveloppé. Des Métropoles au Tiers Monde*, Paris: Maspéro, 1983, 89 (my translation).

Bibliography

Adamolekun, Lapido. (1971) "Bureaucrats and the Senegalese Political Process." *The Journal of Modern African Studies* , Vol. 9, No. 4: 543–559.

Adamson, Walter L. (1980) *Hegemony and Revolution*. Berkeley: University of California Press.

Afrique Contemporaine. (1981) Janvier–février: 20–21.

_____. (1981) Mars–avril: 26–27.

Ake, Claude. (1978) *Revolutionary Pressures in Africa*. London: Zed Press.

_____. (1981) *A Political Economy of Africa*. New York: Longman.

Alliance Démocratique Sénégalaise. (1985) *Plate-forme d'Unité d'Action*.

Amin, Samir. (1969) *Le Monde des Affaires Sénégalais*. Paris: Editions de Minuit.

_____. (1973) *Neo-Colonialism in West Africa*. Harmondsworth: Penguin Books.

_____. (1974) *Accumulation on a World Scale*. New York: Monthly Review Press.

_____. (1981) "The Development of the Senegalese Business Bourgeoisie," 309–321 in Adebayo Adedeji (ed.) *Indigenization of African Economies*. London: Hutchinson University Library.

Anson-Meyer, Monique. (1974) *Mécanismes de l'Exploitation en Afrique. L'Exemple du Sénégal*. La Rochelle: Editions Cujas.

Barker, Jonathan. (1971) "The Paradox of Development. Reflections on a Study of Local-Central Political Relations in Senegal," 47–63 in Michael F. Lofchie (ed.) *The State of the Nations. Constraints on Development in Independent Africa*. Berkeley: University of California Press.

_____. (1973) "Political Factionalism in Senegal." *Canadian Journal of African Studies,* Vol. 7, No. 2: 287–303.

_____. (1977) "Stability and Stagnation: The State in Senegal."

Canadian Journal of African Studies, Vol. 11, No. 1: 23–42.

Barry, Boubacar. (1972) *Le Royaume du Waalo.* Paris: François Maspéro.

_____. (1985) "Les Indépendances Africaines: Origines et Conséquences du Transfert du Pouvoir 1956–1980—Le Sénégal 1960–1980." Colloquium, University of Zimbabwe, January 8–11.

Bates, Robert H. (1981) *Markets and States in Tropical Africa. The Political Basis of Agricultural Policies.* Berkeley: University of California Press.

Bayart, Jean-François. (1985) *L'Etat au Cameroun,* 2nd. Edition. Paris: Presses de la Fondation Nationale des Sciences Politiques.

Behrman, Lucy. (1970) *Muslim Brotherhoods and Politics in Senegal.* Cambridge: Harvard University Press.

Biarnes, Pierre. (1968) "Sénégal: Montée d'un Patronat Africain." *Revue Française d'Etudes Politiques Africaines,* No. 35: 14–16.

_____. (1970) "Sénégal: Les Jeunes au Pouvoir." *Revue Française d'Etudes Politiques Africaines,* No. 5: 9–11.

_____. (1979) "A Propos du Deuxième Congrès du PAI Sénégalais (Dakar—16 et 17 Février 1979)." *Revue Française d'Etudes Politiques Africaines,* No. 160: 60–63.

Bienen, Henry. (1971) "Political Parties and Political Machines in Africa," 195–213 in Michael F. Lofchie (ed.) *The State of the Nations.* Berkeley: University of California Press.

Blanchet, Gilles. (1978) "L'Evolution des Dirigeants Sénégalais de l'Indépendance à 1975." *Cahiers d'Etudes Africaines,* No. 69–70: 49–78.

_____. (1983) *Elites et Changements en Afrique et au Sénégal.* Paris: ORSTOM.

Callaghy, Thomas. (1984) *The State-Society Struggle: Zaire in Comparative Perspective.* New York: Columbia University Press.

_____. (Forthcoming) "The State and the Development of Capitalism in Africa: Some Theoretical and Historical Reflections," to be included in Naomi Chazan and Donald Rothcild (eds.) *Balancing State-Society Relations in Africa.* Boulder: Westview Press.

Cardoso, Fernando Henrique and Faletto, Enzo. (1979) *Dependency and Development in Latin America.* Berkeley: University of California Press.

Cardoso, Fernando Henrique. (1979) "On the Characterization of Authoritarian Regimes in Latin America," 33–57 in David Collier (ed.) *The New Authoritarianism in Latin America .* Princeton: Princeton University Press.

Carnoy, Martin. (1984) *The State and Political Theory .* Princeton: Princeton University Press.

Casswell, N. (1984) "Autopsie de l'ONCAD: La Politique Arachidière au Sénégal, 1966–1980." *Politique Africaine,* No. 14: 39–73.

Chilcote, Ronald H. (1984) *Theories of Development and Underdevelopment.* Boulder: Westview Press.

Club Nation et Développement du Sénégal. (1972) *Club Nation et Développement du Sénégal.* Paris: Présence Africaine.

Coleman, James S., and Carl G. Rosberg. (1971) "African One-Party States and Modernization," 330–354 in Claude E. Welch Jr. (2nd ed.) *Political Modernization.* Belmont, Mass.: Duxbury Press.

Collier, David. (1979) "Overview of the Bureaucratic-Authoritarian Model," 19–32 in David Collier (ed.) *The New Authoritarianism in Latin America.* Princeton: Princeton University Press.

Cooper, Frederick. (1981) "Africa and the World Economy," *The African Studies Review,* Vol. 24, Nos. 2/3: 1–86

Copans, Jean. (1978) "Paysannerie et Politique au Sénégal." *Cahiers d'Etudes Africaines,* No. 69–70: 241–256.

———. (1980) *Les Marabouts de L'Arachide.* Paris: Le Sycomore.

———. (1981) "Les Chercheurs de la Confrérie et la Confrérie des Chercheurs. A Chacun Son Khalife et Marx pour Tous?" *Politique Africaine,* No. 4: 117–121.

Cottingham, Clement. (1970) "Political Consolidation and Centre-Local Relations in Senegal." *Canadian Journal of African Studies,* Vol. 4, No. 1: 101–120.

Coulon, Christian. (1975) "Pouvoir Oligarchique et Mutations Sociales et Politiques au Fouta-Toro," 23–80 in Jean-Louis Balans et al. (eds.) *Autonomie Locale et Intégration Nationale au Sénégal,* Paris: Editions A. Pedone.

———. (1978) "Elections, Factions et Idéologies au Sénégal," 149–186 in Centre d'Etude d'Afrique Noire (ed.) *Aux Urnes l'Afrique! Elections et Pouvoirs en Afrique Noire.* Paris: Editions A. Pedone.

———. (1979) "Les Marabouts Sénégalais et l'Etat." *Revue Françaises de Politiques Africaines,* No. 158: 15–42.

———. (1981) "Les Marabouts Idéologiques." *Politique Africaine,* No. 4: 111–114.

———. (1981) *Le Marabout et le Prince.* Paris: Editions A. Pedone.

———. (1983) *Les Musulmans et le Pouvoir en Afrique Noire.* Paris: Karthala.

Creevey, Lucy. (1985) "Muslim Brotherhoods and Politics in Senegal in 1985." *The Journal of Modern African Studies* , Vol. 23, No. 4: 715–721.

de Benoist, Joseph Roger. (1982) *L'Afrique Occidentale Française de 1944 à 1960.* Dakar: Les Nouvelles Editions Africaines.

Desouches, Christine. (1983) *Le Parti Démocratique Sénégalais.* Paris: Berger-Levrault.

Diagne, Pathé F. (1984) *Sénégal: Crise Economique et Sociale et Devenir de la Démocratie.* Dakar: Sankore.

Diop, Abdoulaye Bara. (1981) *La Société Wolof.* Paris: Karthala.

Diop, Ousman Blondin. (1982) *Les Heritiers d'une Indépendance.* Dakar: Les Nouvelles Editions Africaines.

Diouf, Abdou. (No date) *Le Sursaut National Avec Abdou Diouf.* Dakar: Publications du Parti Socialiste.

_____. (1984) *Rapport de Politique Générale: Le PS, Moteur du Sursaut National*. Dakar: Publications du Parti Socialiste.

_____. (1984) *Allocution D'Ouverture, Séminaire D'Etudes et de Recherches du Comité Central du Parti Socialiste*. Dakar.

_____. (1985) *Rapport Introductif*. Conseil National du Parti Socialiste, Dakar: 11 Mai.

Dos Santos, Theotonio. (1973) "The Structure of Dependence," 109–117 in Charles K. Wilber (1st. ed.) *The Political Economy of Development and Underdevelopment*. New York: Random House.

Dumont, René. (1980) *L'Afrique Etranglée*. Paris: Editions du Seuil.

Emerson, Rupert. (1971) "The Prospects for Democracy in Africa," 239–257 in Michael F. Lofchie (ed.) *The State of the Nations*. Berkeley: University of California Press.

Emmanuel, Arghiri. (1972) *Unequal Exchange*. New York: Monthly Review Press.

Evans, Peter. (1979) *Dependent Development*. Princeton: Princeton University Press.

Fall, Ibrahima. (1977) *Sous-Développement et Démocratie Multipartisane: L'Expérience Sénégalaise*. Dakar: Les Nouvelles Editions Africaines.

Fall, Mar. (1984) "Le Multipartisme et l'Union Nationale au Sénégal?" *Le Mois en Afrique*, No. 217–218: 31–37.

Flynn, Peter. (1974) "Class, Clientelism and Coercion: Some Mechanisms of Internal Dependency and Control." *Journal of Commonwealth Political Studies*, Vol. 12, No. 2: 133–156.

Foltz, William. J. (1964) "Senegal," 16–64 in James S. Coleman and Carl G. Rosberg Jr. (ed.) *Political Parties and National Integration in Tropical Africa*. Berkeley: University of California Press.

_____. (1969) "Le Parti Africain de l'Indépendance: Les Dilemmes d'un Mouvement Communiste en Afrique Occidentale." *Revue Française d'Etudes Politiques Africaines*, No. 45: 8–35.

_____. (1977) "Social Structure and Political Behavior of Senegalese Elites," 242–250 in Steffen W. Schmidt, James C. Scott, Carl Land and Laura Guasti (eds.) *Friends, Followers and Factions*. Berkeley: University of California Press.

Fougeyrollas, Pierre. (1970) *Où Va le Sénégal?* Paris: Editions Anthropos.

Frank, André Gunder. (1979) *Dependent Accumulation and Underdevelopment*. New York: Monthly Review Press.

_____. (1981) *Crisis: In the Third World*. New York: Holmes and Meier Publishers.

French, Howard. (1984) "Diouf Faces Tough Tests." *Africa News*, Vol. 23, No. 21–22: 11–12.

Gautron, Jean-Claude. (1979) "Les Entreprises Publiques, Acteur et Indicateur du Changement Social." *Revue Française d'Etudes Politiques Africaines*, No. 158: 43–62.

Gellar, Sheldon. (1982) *Senegal: An African Nation Between Islam and the West.* Boulder: Westview Press.

_____. (1984) "The Politics of Accommodation: The Evolution of State-Society Relationships in Senegal in the Postcolonial Era." Paper presented at the Twenty-Seventh Annual Meeting of the African Studies Association, Los Angeles, CA.

Gerry, Chris. (1979) "The Crisis of the Self-Employed: Petty Production and Capitalist Production in Dakar," 126–155 in Rita Cruise O'Brien (ed.) *The Political Economy of Underdevelopment: Dependence in Senegal.* Beverly Hills: Sage Publications.

Geschiere, P. (1984) "La Paysannerie Africaine: Est-Elle Captive?" *Politique Africaine.* No. 14: 13–33.

Gramsci, Antonio. (1971) *Selections from Prison Notebooks.* Edited and translated by Quintin Hoare and Geoffrey Nowell Smith. London: Lawrence and Wishart.

Green, Reginald H. (1981) "Magendo in the Political Economy of Uganda." Discussion Paper 164, Institute for Development Studies, University of Sussex.

Gruhn, Isebill V. (1983) "The Recolonization of Africa: International Organizations on the March." *Africa Today,* Vol. 30, No. 4: 37–48.

Guasti, Laura. (1977) "Peru: Clientelism and Internal Control," 422–438 in Steffen W. Schmidt, James C. Scott, Carl Landé and Laura Guasti (eds.) *Friends, Followers, and Factions.* Berkeley: University of California Press.

Hall, Stuart. (1981) "Moving Right." *Socialist Review,* No. 55: 113–137.

Harrison, Paul. (1981) *Inside the Third World* (2nd. ed.). New York: Penguin Books.

Hesseling, Gerti. (1985) *Histoire Politique du Sénégal.* Paris: Karthala.

Hirschman, Albert. (1981) *Essays in Trespassing: Economics to Politics and Beyond.* Cambridge: Cambridge University Press.

Huntington, Samuel P. (1968) *Political Order in Changing Societies.* New Haven: Yale University Press.

_____. (1971) "Political Development and Political Decay," 238–277 in Claude E. Welch Jr. (2nd ed.) *Political Modernization.* Belmont, Mass.: Duxbury Press.

_____. (1981) *American Politics: The Promise of Disharmony.* Cambridge: Harvard University Press.

Hyden, Goran. (1983) *No Shortcuts to Progress.* Berkeley: University of California Press.

Jackson, Robert, and Carl G. Rosberg. (1982) *Personal Rule in Black Africa.* Berkeley: University of California Press.

Jeune Afrique. (1978) 29 Novembre: 31–33.

_____. (1983) 19 Janvier: 24–25.

Johnson, Wesley G. (1971) *The Emergence of Black Politics in Senegal.* Stanford: Stanford University Press.

Kasfir, Nelson. (1984) "State, Magendo, and Class Formation in

Uganda," in Nelson Kasfir (ed.) *State and Class in Africa*, London: Frank Cass, 84–103.

Laclau, Ernesto, and Chantal Mouffe. (1985) *Hegemony and Socialist Strategy*. London: Verso.

Lemarchand, René. (1977) "Political Clientelism and Ethnicity in Tropical Africa," 100–123 in Steffen W. Schmidt, James C. Scott, Carl Landé, and Laura Guasti (eds.) *Friends, Followers and Factions*. Berkeley: University of California Press.

Le Soleil. (1983) 9 Janvier: 1.

_____. (1983) 10 Janvier: 1.

_____. (1983) 28 Février: 1–23.

_____. (1983) 2 Mars: 1–4.

_____. (1983) 8 Mars: 1.

_____. (1985) 29 Avril: 4.

Lewis, Arthur W. (1970) "Beyond African Dictatorship: The Crisis of the One Party State," 83–92 in Marion E. Doro and Newell M. Stultz (eds.) *Governing in Black Africa*. Englewood Cliffs, N.J.: Prentice-Hall.

Leys, Colin. (1965) "What is the Problem About Corruption?" *The Journal of Modern African Studies*, Vol. 3, No. 2: 215–230.

_____. (1982) "African Economic Development in Theory and Practice." *Daedalus*, Vol. 3, No. 2: 99–124.

Liberté. (1985) No. 1, Mars: 12–17.

Lindblom, Charles E. (1977) *Politics and Markets*. New York: Basic Books.

Linz, Juan. (1978) *Crisis, Breakdown and Reequilibration*. Baltimore: The Johns Hopkins University Press.

Lipset, Seymour Martin. (1981) *Political Man*. Baltimore: The Johns Hopkins University Press.

Lofchie, Michael F. (1970) "Representative Government, Bureaucracy, and Political Development: The African Case," 278–294 in Marion E. Doro and Newell M. Stultz (ed.) *Governing in Black Africa*. Englewood Cliffs, N.J.: Prentice-Hall.

_____. (1971) "Political Constraints on African Development," 9-18 in Michael F. Lofchie (ed.) *The State of the Nations*. Berkeley: University of California Press.

Ly, Abdoulaye. (1981) *L'Emergence du Néocolonialisme au Sénégal*. Dakar: Editions Xamle.

_____. (1984?) *Sur le Présidentialisme Néocolonial au Sénégal. Pour un Positionnement Objectif*. Dakar: AND–DEF/MRDN.

Mackintosh, Maureen. (1979) "The Political Economy of Industrial Wages in Senegal," 156–174 in Rita Cruise O'Brien (ed.) *The Political Economy of Underdevelopment: Dependence in Senegal*. Beverly Hills: Sage Publications.

Macpherson, C. B. (1977) *The Life and Times of Liberal Democracy*. New York: Oxford University Press.

Markovitz, Irving Leonard. (1969) *Léopold Sédar Senghor and the*

Politics of Négritude. New York: Atheneum.

_____. (1970) "Traditional Social Structure, The Islamic Brotherhoods, and Political Development in Senegal." *The Journal of Modern African Studies*, Vol. 8, No. 1: 73–96.

_____(ed.) (Forthcoming) *Studies in Power and Class in Africa*. New York: Oxford University Press.

Marx, Karl. (1972) *The Marx-Engels Reader*. Edited by Robert C. Tucker. New York: W. W. Norton & Company.

Mathias, Gilberto, and Pierre Salama. (1983) *L'Etat Surdéveloppé. Des Métropoles au Tiers Monde*. Paris: Maspéro.

Miliband, Ralph. (1977) *Marxism and Politics*. New York: Oxford University Press.

_____. (1983) *Class Power and State Power*. London: Verso.

Moore, Barrington, Jr. (1978) *Injustice: The Social Bases of Obedience and Revolt*. White Plains: M. E. Sharpe.

Mulot, Francis. (1979) "Syndicalisme et Politique au Sénégal (1968/69-1976)." *Revue Française d'Etudes Politiques Africaines*, No. 158: 63–90.

Myrdal, Gunnar. (1970) *The Challenge of World Poverty*. New York: Vintage Books.

Ndiaye, Jean-Pierre. (1976) *Monde Noir et Destin Politique* . Dakar: Les Nouvelles Editions Africaines.

Nkrumah, Kwame. (1961) *I Speak of Freedom: A Statement of African Ideology*. New York: Praeger.

Nyerere, Julius. (1967) *Freedom and Unity*. Dar es Salaam: Oxford University Press.

_____. (1968) *Freedom and Socialism*. London: Oxford University Press.

_____. (1973) *Freedom and Development*. New York: Oxford University Press.

Nzouankeu, Jacques Mariel. (1983) "L'Evolution des Partis Politiques Sénégalais Depuis le 22 Juillet 1983." *Revue des Institutions Politiques et Administratives du Sénégal*, No. 8: 773-783.

_____. (1984) *Les Partis Politiques Sénégalais*. Dakar: Editions Claireafrique.

O'Brien, Donal B. Cruise. (1967) "Political Opposition in Senegal: 1960–67." *Government and Opposition*, Vol. 2, No. 4: 557–566.

_____. (1971) *The Mourides of Senegal*. Oxford: Oxford University Press.

_____. (1975) *Saints and Politicians*. Cambridge: Cambridge University Press.

_____. (1978) "Senegal," 173–188 in John Dunn (ed.) *West African States: Failure and Promise*. Cambridge: Cambridge University Press.

_____. (1979) "Ruling Class and Peasantry in Senegal, 1960–1976: The Politics of a Monocrop Economy," 209–227 in Rita Cruise O'Brien (ed.) *The Political Economy of Underdevelopment:*

Dependence in Senegal. Beverly Hills: Sage Publications.

_____. (1983) "Senegal's Elections: What Went Wrong." *West Africa,* 21 March: 714–715.

_____. (1983) "Les Elections Sénégalaises du 27 Février 1983." *Politique Africaine,* No. 11: 7–12.

_____. (1984) "Des Bienfaits de l'Inégalité: L'Etat et l'Economie Rurale au Sénégal." *Politique Africaine,* No. 14: 34–38.

O'Brien, Rita Cruise (ed.). (1979) *The Political Economy of Underdevelopment: Dependence in Senegal.* Beverly Hills: Sage Publications.

_____. (1979) "Foreign Ascendance in the Economy and State: The French and Lebanese," 100–125 in Rita Cruise O'Brien (ed.) *The Political Economy of Underdevelopment: Dependence in Senegal.* Beverly Hills: Sage Publications.

O'Donnell, Guillermo. (1979) "Tensions in the Bureaucratic–Authoritarian State and the Question of Democracy," 285–318 in David Collier (ed.) *The New Authoritarianism in Latin America .* Princeton: Princeton University Press.

Poulantzas, Nicos. (1974) *Political Power and Social Classes.* London: New Left Books.

_____. (1980) *State, Power, Socialism.* London: Verso Edition.

Przeworski, Adam. (1980) "Social Democracy as a Historical Phenomenon." *New Left Review,* No. 122: 27–58.

Revue des Institutions Politiques et Administratives du Sénégal (RIPAS) . (1982), Octobre–décembre, No. 5.

Revue des Institutions Politiques et Administrative du Sénégal (RIPAS). (1983) Janvier–juin, Nos. 6–7.

Revue des Institutions Politiques et Administratives du Sénégal (RIPAS) . (1983) Octobre–décembre, No. 8.

Rocheteau, Guy. (1982) *Pouvoir Financier et Indépendance Economique en Afrique: Le Cas du Sénégal.* Paris: Karthala.

Rodney, Walter. (1972) *How Europe Underdeveloped Africa.* Washington: Howard University Press.

Rostow, Walter. (1960) *The Stages of Economic Growth.* Cambridge: Cambridge University Press.

Rouquié, Alain. (1978) "La Dynamique des Elections Sans Risque où la Voie Africaine de l'Etat," 217–228 in Centre d'étude d'Afrique Noire (ed.) *Aux Urnes l'Afrique! Elections et Pouvoirs en Afrique Noire.* Paris: Editions A. Pedone.

Samoff, Joel. (1982) "Class, Class Conflict, and the State in Africa." *Political Science Quarterly,* Vol. 97, No. 1: 105–127.

Sandbrook, Richard. (1972) "Patrons, Clients, and Factions: New Dimensions of Conflict Analysis in Africa." *Canadian Journal of Political Science,* Vol. 5, No. 1: 104–119.

_____. (1982) *The Politics of Basic Needs.* Toronto: Toronto University Press.

_____. (1985) *The Politics of Africa's Economic Stagnation.* New

York: Cambridge University Press.

Sassoon, Anne Showstack (ed.). (1982) *Approaches to Gramsci*. London: Writers and Readers.

_____. (1982a) "Passive Revolution and the Politics of Reform," 127–148 in Anne Showstack Sassoon (ed.) *Approaches to Gramsci*. London: Writers and Readers.

Saul, John S. (1979) *The State and Revolution in Eastern Africa*. New York: Monthly Review Press.

Savane, Landing. (1981). *La Situation Economique du Sénégal et le FMI*. Dakar: AND–JEF/MRDN.

Schmidt, Steffen W., et al. (1977). *Friends, Followers and Factions*. Berkeley: University of California Press.

Schumacher, Edward J. (1975) *Politics, Bureaucracy, and Rural Development in Senegal*. Berkeley: University of California Press.

Schumpeter, Joseph. (1975) *Capitalism, Socialism and Democracy*, 3rd. ed. New York: Harper Brothers.

Scott, James C. (1977) "Patron-Client Politics and Political Change in Southeast Asia," 123–146 in Steffen W. Schmidt, James C. Scott, Carl Landé, and Laura Guasti (eds.) *Friends, Followers, and Factions*. Berkeley: University of California Press.

_____, and Kerkvliet, Benedict. (1977) "How Traditional Rural Patrons Lose Legitimacy: A Theory with Special Reference to Southeast Asia," 439–458 in Steffen W. Schmidt, James C. Scott, Carl Landé, and Laura Guasti (eds.) *Friends, Followers, and Factions*. Berkeley: University of California Press.

Sen, Amartya. (1982) *Poverty and Famines*. Oxford: Oxford Universty Press.

Senghor, Léopold Sédar. (1964) *Liberté I: Négritude et Humanisme*. Paris: Editions du Seuil.

_____. (1971) *Liberté II: Nation et Voie Africaine du Socialisme*. Paris: Editions du Seuil.

_____. (1972) *Rapport de Politique Générale: Le Plan du Décollage Economique ou la Participation Responsable Comme Moteur du Développement*. Dakar: Grande Imprimerie Africaine.

_____. (1976) *Pour une Société Sénégalaise Socialiste et Démocratique*. Dakar: Les Nouvelles Editions Africaines.

_____. (1977) *Liberté III: Négritude et Civilisation de l'Universel*. Paris: Editions du Seuil.

_____. (1980) *Léopold Sédar Senghor: La Poésie de l'Action. Conversations avec Mohamed Aziza*. Paris: Stock.

_____. (1983) *Liberté IV: Socialisme et Planification*. Paris: Editions du Seuil.

Shaw, Timothy. (1982) "Beyond Neo-colonialism: Varieties of Corporatism in Africa." *The Journal of Modern African Studies*, Vol. 20, No. 2: 239–261.

Sine, Babacar. (1983) *Le Marxisme Devant les Société Africaines*

Contemporaines. Dakar: Présence Africaine.

_____. (1984) "Abdou Diouf entre Deux Fronts," *Le Soleil,* 20 juillet: 1–5.

Sklar, Richard L. (1983) "Democracy in Africa." *African Studies Review,* Vol. 26, Nos. 3/4: 11–24.

Stepan, Alfred. (1978) *The State and Society.* Princeton: Princeton University Press.

Swainson, Nicola. (1980) *The Development of Corporate Capitalism in Kenya, 1918–1977.* Berkeley: University of California Press.

Sylla, A. (1982) "De la Grève à la Réforme: Luttes Enseignantes et Crise Sociale au Sénégal." *Politique Africaine,* No. 8: 61–73.

Takusaan. (1983) 2 Mars: 2–15.

Terrisse, André. (1970) "Aspects du Malaise Paysan au Sénégal." *Revue Française d'Etudes Politiques Africaines,* No. 55: 79–91.

Therborn, Goran. (1979) "The Travail of Latin American Democracy." *New Left Review,* Nos. 113–114: 71–109.

_____. (1980) *What Does the Ruling Class Do When It Rules?* London: Verso Editions.

_____. (1983) "The Rule of Capital and the Rise of Democracy," 261–271 in David Held et al. (ed.) *States and Societies.* New York: New York University Press.

Thibaud, Paul. (1963) "Document: Dia, Senghor et le Socialisme Africain." *Esprit,* No. 320: 332–348.

Thomas, Clive Y. (1974) *Dependence and Transformation.* New York: Monthly Review Press.

_____. (1984) *The Rise of the Authoritarian State in Peripheral Societies .* New York: Monthly Review Press.

Vansina, Jan. (1982) "Mwasi's Trial." *Daedalus,* Vol. 3, No. 2: 49–72.

Wade, Abdoulaye. (1967) "La Doctrine Economique du Mouridisme." *Annales Africaines:* 175–208.

Wallerstein, Immanuel. (1966) "The Decline of the Party in Single-Party African States," 201–214 in Joseph La Palombara and Myron Weiner (eds.) *Political Parties and Political Development.* Princeton: Princeton University Press.

_____. (1971) "The Range of Choice: Constraints on the Policies of Governments of Contemporary African Independent States," 19–33 in Michael F. Lofchie (ed.) *The State of the Nations.* Berkeley: University of California Press.

_____. (1979) *The Capitalist World Economy .* Cambridge: Cambridge University Press.

Weber, Max. (1978) *Economy and Society.* Edited by Guenther Roth and Claus Wittich. Berkeley: University of California Press.

West Africa. (1978) 20 February: 327.

_____. (1978) 6 March: 421.

_____. (1981) 19 January: 102–104.

_____. (1981) 23 February: 365.

_____. (1981) 25 May: 1142–1143.

_____. (1981) 20 July: 1638–1640.

_____. (1981) 27 July: 1689–1692.

_____. (1982) 25 January: 213–217.

_____. (1982) 2 August: 1984–1985.

_____. (1983) 21 February: 460–461.

_____. (1983) 28 February: 534–537.

_____. (1983) 7 March: 589–590.

_____. (1983) 14 March: 644–645.

_____. (1983) 28 March: 766–767.

Worsley, Peter. (1984) *The Three Worlds*. Chicago: The University of Chicago Press.

Young, Crawford. (1982) "Patterns of Social Conflict: State, Class, and Ethnicity." *Daedalus*, Vol. 3, No. 2: 71–98.

_____. (1982) *Ideology and Development in Africa* . New Haven: Yale University Press.

Zolberg, Aristide R. (1966) *Creating Political Order*. Chicago: Rand McNally.

Zuccarelli, François. (1970) *Un Parti Politique Africain: L'Union Progressiste Sénégalaise*. Paris: Pichon et Durand–Auzias.

_____. (1976) "L'Evolution Récente de la Vie Politique Au Sénégal." *Revue Française d'Etudes Politiques Africaines*, No. 127: 85–102.

Periodicals and Newspapers

AND–SOPI	*Liberte*	*L'Unité*
Daan Doole	*Monsarew*	*Voix du Peuple*
Le Démocrate	*Le Politicien*	*West Africa*
Le Devoir	*Reew Mi*	*Xarebi*
Fagaru	*Renouveau*	*Yaakaar*
Jaay Doole	*Le Soleil*	
Jeune Afrique	*Takusaan*	

Personal Interviews

Personalities of the Government

President Abdou Diouf, November 8, 1985.

Foreign Minister Ibrahima Fall, November 12, 1985.

Mamadou Faye, Permanent Secretary of the Parti socialiste, May 11, 1985.

President Léopold Sédar Senghor, November 11, 1985.

Personalities of the Opposition

Abdoulaye Bathily, Secretary General of the Ligue démocratique/ Mouvement pour le travail, November 13, 1985.

Amath Dansoko, Secretary General of the Parti de l'indépendance et du travail-Sénégal, April 29, 1985.

Abdoulaye Ly, May 8, 1985.

Landing Savane, Secretary General of the AND–JEF/MRDN, April 30, 1985.

Abdoulaye Wade, General Secretary of the Parti démocratique du Sénégal, April 30 and May 7, 1985.

Index